Berlitz®

French

phrase book & dictionary

Berlitz Publishing
New York London Singapore

Contacting the Editors

Every effort has been made to provide accurate information in this publication, but changes are inevitable. The publisher cannot be responsible for any resulting loss, inconvenience or injury. We would appreciate it if readers would call our attention to any errors or outdated information. We also welcome your suggestions; if you come across a relevant expression not in our phrase book, please contact us at: **comments@berlitzpublishing.com**

All Rights Reserved
© 2018 Apa Digital (CH) AG and Apa Publications (UK) Ltd.
Berlitz Trademark Reg. U.S. Patent Office and other countries. Marca Registrada. Used under license from Berlitz Investment Corporation.

Twelfth Printing: March 2018
Printed in China

Editor: Helen Fanthorpe
Translation: updated by Wordbank
Cover Design: Rebeka Davies
Interior Design: Beverley Speight
Picture Researcher: Tom Smyth
Cover Photos: all images iStock and Shutterstock

Interior Photos: Kevin Cummins/APA 1, 12, 27, 39, 61, 81, 90, 94, 97, 98, 100, 112, 116, 119, 122, 125, 127, 128, 131, 132, 135, 144, 147, 165; iStockphoto 21, 146, 153, 154, 157, 160; Britta Jaschinski/APA 55, 68, 150; Lucy Johnston/APA 16, 182; James MacDonald/APA 58; Ilpo Musto/APA 115, 142; Sylvaine Poitau/APA 42, 47, 73, 76, 82, 85, 87, 89, 93, 137, 149; James Wadey/APA 139, 141.

Distribution

UK, Ireland and Europe
Apa Publications (UK) Ltd
sales@insightguides.com
United States and Canada
Ingram Publisher Services
ips@ingramcontent.com
Australia and New Zealand
Woodslane
info@woodslane.com.au
Southeast Asia
Apa Publications (SN) Pte
singaporeoffice@insightguides.com

Worldwide
Apa Publications (UK) Ltd
sales@insightguides.com

Special Sales, Content Licensing, and CoPublishing
Discounts available for bulk quantities. We can create special editions, personalized jackets, and corporate imprints. sales@insightguides.com; www.insightguides.biz

Contents

Pronunciation	7	Vowels	8
Consonants	7	How to use this Book	10

Survival

Arrival & Departure	**13**	Asking Directions	33
ESSENTIAL	13	Parking	34
Border Control	13	Breakdown & Repair	35
		Accidents	35
Money	**14**		
ESSENTIAL	14	**Places to Stay**	**36**
At the Bank	15	ESSENTIAL	36
		Somewhere to Stay	37
Getting Around	**17**	At the Hotel	38
ESSENTIAL	17	Price	39
Tickets	18	Preferences	40
Plane	19	Questions	40
Airport Transfer	19	Problems	42
Checking In	21	Checking Out	43
Luggage	23	Renting	44
Finding your Way	23	Domestic Items	45
Train	24	At the Hostel	46
Departures	25	Going Camping	47
On Board	25		
Bus	26	**Communications**	**48**
Metro	27	ESSENTIAL	48
Boat & Ferry	28	Online	50
Taxi	29	Social Media	51
Bicycle & Motorbike	31	Phone	53
Car Hire	31	Telephone Etiquette	54
Fuel Station	32	Fax	56
		Post	56

Food & Drink

Eating Out 59
ESSENTIAL 59
Where to Eat 60
Reservations & Preferences 60
How to Order 62
Cooking Methods 64
Dietary Requirements 64
Dining with Children 65
How to Complain 66
Paying 66

Meals & Cooking 67
Breakfast 68
Appetizers 69
Soup 70
Fish & Seafood 72
Meat & Poultry 74

Vegetables & Staples 75
Fruit 77
Cheese 78
Dessert 79
Sauces & Condiments 80
At the Market 80
In the Kitchen 83

Drinks 84
ESSENTIAL 84
Non-alcoholic Drinks 85
Apéritifs, Cocktails & Liqueurs 86
Beer 87
Wine 87

On the Menu 89

People

Conversation 103
ESSENTIAL 103
Language Difficulties 104
Making Friends 105
Travel Talk 106
Personal 106
Work & School 108
Weather 108

Romance 109
ESSENTIAL 109
The Dating Game 109
Accepting & Rejecting 110
Getting Intimate 111
Sexual Preferences 111

Leisure Time

Sightseeing **113**
ESSENTIAL 113
Tourist Information 113
On Tour 114
Seeing the Sights 114
Religious Sites 116

Shopping **117**
ESSENTIAL 117
At the Shops 117
Ask an Assistant 118
Personal Preferences 120
Paying & Bargaining 121
Making a Complaint 122
Services 123
Hair & Beauty 123
Antiques 125
Clothing 125
Colors 127
Clothes & Accessories 127

Fabric 129
Shoes 129
Sizes 130
Newsagent & Tobacconist 130
Photography 131
Souvenirs 132

Sport & Leisure **134**
ESSENTIAL 134
Watching Sport 134
Playing Sport 136
At the Beach/Pool 136
Winter Sports 138
Out in the Country 139

Going Out **141**
ESSENTIAL 141
Entertainment 141
Nightlife 143

Special Requirements

Business Travel **145**
ESSENTIAL 145
On Business 145

Traveling with Children **148**
ESSENTIAL 148
Out & About 148

Baby Essentials 149
Babysitting 151
Health & Emergency 151

Disabled Travelers **152**
ESSENTIAL 152
Asking for Assistance 152

In an Emergency

Emergencies **155**
ESSENTIAL 155

Police **156**
ESSENTIAL 156
Crime & Lost Property 156

Health **158**
ESSENTIAL 158
Finding a Doctor 158
Symptoms 158
Conditions 159
Treatment 161
Hospital 161
Dentist 162
Gynecologist 162
Optician 162
Payment & Insurance 163
Pharmacy 163
ESSENTIAL 163
What to Take 164

Basic Supplies 165

The Basics **167**
Grammar 167
Numbers 173
ESSENTIAL 173
Ordinal Numbers 174
Time 175
ESSENTIAL 175
Days 176
ESSENTIAL 176
Dates 176
Months 176
Seasons 177
Public Holidays 177
Conversion Tables 178
Kilometers to Miles
Conversions 179
Measurement 179
Temperature 179
Oven Temperature 179

Dictionary

English-French
Dictionary 181

French-English
Dictionary 203

Pronunciation

This section is designed to make you familiar with the sounds of French using our simplified phonetic transcription. You'll find the pronunciation of the French letters and sounds explained below, together with their 'imitated' equivalents. This system is used throughout the phrase book; simply read the pronunciation as if it were English, noting any special rules below.

In French, all syllables are pronounced the same, with no extra stress on any particular syllable. The French language contains nasal vowels, which are indicated in the pronunciation by a vowel symbol followed by an N. This N should not be pronounced strongly, but it is there to show the nasal quality of the previous vowel. A nasal vowel is pronounced simultaneously through the mouth and the nose.

In French, the final consonants of words are not always pronounced. When a word ending in a consonant is followed with a word beginning with a vowel, the two words are often run together. The consonant is therefore pronounced as if it begins the following word.

Example	Pronunciation
comment	*koh•mawN*
Comment allez-vous ?	*koh•mawN tah•lay-voo*

Consonants

Letter	Approximate Pronunciation	Symbol	Example	Pronunciation
cc	1. before e, i, like cc in accident	**ks**	**accessible**	*ahk•seh•see•bluh*
	2. elsewhere, like cc in accommodate	**k**	**d'accord**	*dah•kohr*
ch	like sh in shut	**sh**	**chercher**	*shehr•shay*
ç	like s in sit	**s**	**ça**	*sah*

Letter	Approximate Pronunciation	Symbol	Example	Pronunciation
g	1. before e, i, y, like s in pleasure	zh	manger	*mawN•zhay*
	2. before a, o, u, like g in go	g	garçon	*gahr•sohN*
h	always silent		homme	*ohm*
j	like s in pleasure	zh	jamais	*zhah•may*
qu	like k in kill	k	qui	*kee*
r	rolled in the back of the mouth, like gargling	r	rouge	*roozh*
w	usually like v in voice	v	wagon	*vah•gohN*

B, c, d, f, k, l, m, n, p, s, t, v, x and z are pronounced as in English.

Vowels

Letter	Approximate Pronunciation	Symbol	Example	Pronunciation
a, à, â	between the a in hat and the a in father	ah	mari	*mah•ree*
e	sometimes like a in about	uh	je	*zhuh*
è, ê, e	like e in get	eh	même	*mehm*
é, ez	like a in late	ay	été	*ay•tay*
i	like ee in meet	ee	il	*eel*
o, ô	generally like o in roll	oh	donner	*doh•nay*
u	like ew in dew	ew	une	*ewn*

Sounds spelled with two or more letters

Letter	Approximate Pronunciation	Symbol	Example	Pronunciation
ai, ay, aient, ais, ait	like a in late	ay	j'ai vais	*zhay* *vay*
aî, ei	like e in get	eh	chaîne peine	*shehn* *pehn*
(e)au	similar to o	oh	chaud	*shoh*
eu, eû, œu	like u in fur but short like a puff of air	uh	euro	*uh•roh*
euil, euille	like uh + y	uhy	feuille	*fuhy*
ail, aille	like ie in tie	ie	taille	*tie*
ille	1. like yu in yucca 2. like eel	eeyuh eel	famille ville	*fah-meeyuh* *veel*
oi, oy	like w followed by the a in hat	wah	moi	*mwah*
ou, oû	like o in move or oo in hoot	oo	nouveau	*noo•voh*
ui	approximately like wee in between	wee	traduire	*trah•dweer*

There are approximately 129 million French speakers worldwide. French is an official language in 30 countries and the United Nations. French is spoken by 4 million people in Belgium, 7 million in Canada, 60.5 million in France and 1.3 million in Switzerland. It is also an official language of 22 African nations.

How to use this Book

Sometimes you see two alternatives separated by a slash. Choose the one that's right for your situation.

ESSENTIAL

I'm on vacation /business.	**Je suis en vacances/voyage d'affaires.** zhuh swee zawN vah•kawNs/ vwah•yahzh dah•fehr
I'm going to...	**Je vais à/aux...** zhuh vay ah/oh...
I'm staying at the...Hotel.	**Je reste à l'hôtel...** zhuh rehst ah loh•tehl...

Words you may see are shown in YOU MAY SEE boxes.

YOU MAY SEE...

Douanes	customs
Articles Hors Taxes	duty-free goods
Produits À Déclarer	goods to declare

Any of the words or phrases listed can be plugged into the sentence below.

Tickets

A...ticket.	**Un billet pour...** uhN bee•yay poor...
one-way	**un aller simple** uhN nah•lay sehN•pluh
round-trip [return]	**un aller-retour** uhN nah•lay•ruh•toor
first class	**première classe** pruh•meeyehr klahs
economy class	**classe économique** klah say•koh•noh•meek

French phrases appear in purple.

Read the simplified pronunciation as if it were English. For more on pronunciation, see page 7.

The Dating Game

Can I join you?   **Puis-je me joindre à vous?** *pwee-zhuh muh zhwehN•druh ah voo*

You're very attractive.   **Vous êtes très beau m /belle f** *voo zeht tray boh m /behl f*

For Communications, see page 48.

Related phrases can be found by going to the page number indicated.

When different gender forms apply, the masculine form is followed by *m*; feminine by *f*

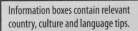

When addressing someone, it is polite to include a title: **monsieur** for a man or **madame** for a woman, even if you suspect she is not married. **Mademoiselle** is used only when addressing young girls.

Information boxes contain relevant country, culture and language tips.

Expressions you may hear are shown in You May Hear boxes.

YOU MAY HEAR...

Je parle un peu anglais.
zhuh pahrl uhN puh awN•glay

I only speak a little English.

Color-coded side bars identify each section of the book.

Survival

Arrival & Departure   13
Money   14
Getting Around   17
Places to Stay   36
Communications   48

Arrival & Departure

ESSENTIAL

I'm on vacation [holiday]/business.	**Je suis en vacances/voyage d'affaires.** *zhuh swee zawN vah•kawNs/vwah•yahzh dah•fehr*
I'm going to...	**Je vais à/aux...** *zhuh vay ah/oh...*
I'm staying at the...Hotel.	**Je reste à l'hôtel...** *zhuh rehst ah loh•tehl...*

For when to use à or aux, see page 173.

YOU MAY HEAR...

Votre passeport, s'il vous plaît. *voh•truh pahs•pohr seel voo play*	Your passport, please.
Quel est le but de votre visite ? *keh lay luh bewt duh voh•truh vee•zeet*	What's the purpose of your visit?
Où restez-vous ? *oo rehs•tay•voo*	Where are you staying?
Combien de temps restez-vous ? *kohN•beeyehN duh tawN rehs•tay•voo*	How long are you staying?
Avec qui êtes-vous ? *ah•vehk kee eht•voo*	Who are you here with?

Border Control

I'm just passing through.	**Je suis juste en transit.** *zhuh swee zhews tawN trawN•zeet*
I'd like to declare...	**Je voudrais déclarer...** *zhuh voo•dray day•klah•ray...*
I have nothing to declare.	**Je n'ai rien à déclarer.** *zhuh nay reeyehN nah day•klah•ray*

YOU MAY HEAR...

Rien à déclarer ?
reeyehN nah day•klah•ray

Anything to declare?

Vous devez payer la taxe sur ceci.
voo duh•vay pay•yay lah tahks sewr suh•see

You must pay duty on this.

Ouvrez ce sac.
oo•vray suh sahk

Open this bag.

YOU MAY SEE...

DOUANES	customs
ARTICLES HORS TAXES	duty-free goods
PRODUITS À DÉCLARER	goods to declare
RIEN À DÉCLARER	nothing to declare
CONTRÔLE DE PASSEPORT	passport control
POLICE	police

Money

ESSENTIAL

Where's...?	**Où est...?** *oo ay...*
the ATM	**le distributeur automatique de billets** *luh dee•stree•bew•tuhr oh•toh•mah•teek duh bee•yay*
the bank	**la banque** *lah bawNk*
the currency exchange office	**le bureau de change** *luh bew•roh duh shawNzh*

When does the bank open/close?	**Quand est-ce que la banque ouvre/ ferme ?** *kawN tehs kuh lah bawNk oo·vruh/fehrm*
I'd like to change dollars/pounds into euros.	**Je voudrais échanger des dollars/livres sterling en euros.** *zhuh voo·dray ay·shawN·zhay day doh·lahr/lee·vruh stayr·leeng awN nuh·roh*
I'd like to cash traveler's cheques.	**Je voudrais encaisser des chèques de voyages.** *zhuh voo·dray awN·kay·say day shehk duh vwah·yahzh*

At the Bank

I'd like to change money/get a cash advance.	**Je voudrais changer de l'argent/obtenir une avance en liquide.** *zhuh voo·dray shawN·zhay duh lahr·zhawN/ohb·tuh·neer ewn ah·vawNs awN lee·keed*
What's the exchange rate/fee?	**Quel est le taux de/prix du change ?** *keh lay luh toh duh/pree dew shawNzh*
I think there's mistake.	**Je pense qu'il y a une erreur.** *zhuh pawNs a keel·yah ewn ay·ruhr*
I lost my traveler's cheques.	**J'ai perdu mes chèques de voyages.** *zhay pehr·dew may shehk duh vwah·yahzh*
The ATM ate my card.	**Le distributeur automatique de billets a avalé ma carte.** *luh dee·stree·bew·tuhr oh·toh·mah·teek duh bee·yay ah ah·vah·lay mah kahrt*
My card...	**Ma carte...** *mah kahrt...*
was lost	**a été perdue** *ah ay·tay pehr·dew*
was stolen	**a été volée** *ah ay·tay voh·lay*
doesn't work	**ne fonctionne pas** *nuh fohNk·seeyohn pah*

For Numbers, see page 173.

At some banks, cash can be obtained from ATMs with Visa™, Eurocard™, American Express® and many other international cards. Instructions are often given in English. Banks with a **Change** sign will exchange foreign currency. You can also change money at travel agencies and hotels, but the rate will not be as good. Remember to bring your passport when you want to change money.

YOU MAY SEE...

INSÉREZ LA CARTE ICI	insert card here
ANNULER	cancel
EFFACER	clear
VALIDER	enter
CODE SECRET	PIN
RETRAIT	withdrawal
DU COMPTE COURANT	from checking [current] account
DU COMPTE ÉPARGNE	from savings
REÇU	receipt

Getting Around

ESSENTIAL

How do I get to town?	**Comment vais-je en ville ?** *koh•mawN vay•zhuh awN veel*
Where's...?	**Où est...?** *oo ay...*
the airport	**l'aéroport** *lah•ay•roh•pohr*
the train station	**la gare** *lah gahr*
the bus station	**la gare routière** *lah gahr roo•tee•yehr*
the Metro station	**le métro** *luh may•troh*
Is it far from here?	**C'est loin d'ici ?** *say lwehN dee•see*
Where do I buy a ticket?	**Où puis-je acheter un billet ?** *oo pwee•zhuh a ah•shtay uhN bee•yay*
A one-way/return-trip ticket to...	**Un billet aller simple/aller-retour...** *uhN bee•yay ah•lay sehN•pluh/ah•lay•ruh•toor...*
How much?	**Combien ça coûte ?** *kohN•beeyehN sah koot*
Which gate/line?	**Quelle porte/ligne ?** *kehl pohrt/lee•nyuh*
Which platform?	**Quel quai ?** *kehl kay*
Where can I get taxi?	**Où puis-je prendre un taxi ?** *oo pwee•zhuh a prawN•druh uhN tahk•see*
Take me to this address.	**Conduisez-moi à cette adresse.** *kohN•dwee•zay•mwah ah seh tah•drehs*
Can I have a map?	**Puis-je avoir une carte ?** *pwee•zhuh ah•vwahr ewn kahrt*

Tickets

When's…to Paris?	**Quand est…pour Paris ?**
	kawN tay…poor pah•ree
the (first) bus	**le (premier) bus** *luh (pruh•meeyay) bews*
the (next) flight	**le (prochain) vol** *luh (proh•shehN) vohl*
the (last) train	**le (dernier) train** *luh (dehr•neeyay) trehN*
Where do I buy	**Où puis-je acheter un billet ?**
a ticket?	*oo pwee•zhuh ah•shtay uhN bee•yay*
One/Two ticket(s).	**Un/Deux billet(s).** *uhN/duh bee•yay*
For today/tomorrow.	**Pour aujourd'hui/demain.**
	poor oh•zhoor•dwee/duh•mehN
A…ticket.	**Un billet…** *uhN bee•yay…*
one-way	**aller simple** *nah•lay sehN•pluh*
return trip	**aller-retour** *nah•lay•ruh•toor*
first class	**première classe** *pruh•meeyehr klahs*
business class	**classe affaire** *klahs ah•fehr*
economy class	**classe économique** *klah say•koh•noh•meek*
How much?	**Combien ça coûte ?** *kohN•beeyehN sah koot*
Is there a	**Y-a-t-il une réduction pour…?**
discount for…?	*yah•teel ewn ray•dewk•see•yohN poor…*
children	**les enfants** *lay zawN•fawN*
students	**les étudiants** *lay zay•tew•dee•yawN*
senior citizens	**les seniors** *lay say•nyohr*
tourists	**les touristes** *lay too•reehst*
The express bus/	**Le bus direct/L'express, s'il vous plaît.**
express train, please.	*luh bews dee•rehkt/lehk•sprehs seel voo play*
The local bus/train,	**Le bus/train régional, s'il vous plaît.**
please.	*luh bews/trehN ray•zheeyoh•nahl seel voo play*
I have an e-ticket.	**J'ai un billet électronique.**
	zhay uhN bee•yay ay•lehk•troh•neek

Can I buy a ticket on the bus/train?	**Puis-je acheter un billet dans le bus/train ?** _pwee•zhuh ah•shtay uhN bee•yay dawN luh bews/ trehN_
Do I have to stamp the ticket before boarding?	**Dois-je composter mon billet avant de monter ?** _dwah•zhuh kohN•poh•stay mohN bee•yay ah•vawN duh mohN•tay_
How long is this ticket valid?	**Jusqu'à quand le billet est-il valable ?** _zhew•skah kawN luh bee•yay eh•teel vah•lah•bluh_
Can I return on the same ticket?	**Puis-je utiliser le même billet pour le retour ?** _pwee•zhuh ew•tee•lee•zay luh mehm bee•yay poor luh rhuh•toor_
I'd like to... my reservation.	**Je voudrais...ma réservation.** _zhuh voo•dray...mah ray•zehr•vah•seeyohN_
cancel	**annuler** _ah•new•lay_
change	**échanger** _ay•shawN•zhay_
confirm	**confirmer** _kohN•feer•may_

For Time, see page 175.

Plane

Airport Transfer

How much is a taxi to the airport?	**Combien coûte le trajet en taxi jusqu'à l'aéroport ?** _kohN•beeyehN koot luh trah•zhay awN tahk•see zhew•skah lah•ay•roh•pohr_
To...Airport, please.	**À l'aéroport de..., s'il vous plaît.** _ah lah•ay•roh•pohr duh... seel voo play_
My flight leaves at...	**Mon vol part à...** _mohN vohl pahr ah..._
I'm in a rush.	**Je suis pressé _m_ /pressée _f_.** _zhuh swee preh•say_
My airline is...	**Ma compagnie aérienne est...** _mah kohN•pah•nee ah•ay•ree•yeh nay..._

Can you take an alternate route?	**Pouvez-vous prendre une route différente ?**
	poo•vay•voo prawN•druh ewn root dee•fay•rawNt
Can you drive faster/slower?	**Pouvez-vous conduire plus/moins vite ?**
	poo•vay•voo kohN•dweer plew/mwehN veet

France has more than 20 main airports. Paris's two airports are Roissy-Charles de Gaulle, located 15 miles (23 km) north of the city, and Orly, located 9 miles (14 km) south of the city. Air France is France's principal domestic airline, with services between major cities: Paris, Lille, Lyon, Strasbourg, Grenoble, Bordeaux, Clermond-Ferrand, Nantes, Marseilles, Nice, Toulouse and more.

YOU MAY HEAR...

Quelle compagnie aérienne prenez-vous ? *kehl kohN•pah•nee ah•ay•ree•yehn pruh•nay•voo*	What airline are you flying?
Nationale ou internationale ? *nah•seeyoh•nahl oo ehN•tehr•nah•seeyoh•nahl*	Domestic or international?
Quel terminal ? *kehl tehr•mee•nahl*	What terminal?

YOU MAY SEE...

LES ARRIVÉES	arrivals
LES DÉPARTS	departures
RETRAIT DES BAGAGES	baggage claim

↑ ✈ 74-82
Departure Gates
Portes d'embarquement

SÉCURITÉ	security
VOLS NATIONAUX	domestic flights
VOLS INTERNATIONAUX	international flights
ENREGISTREMENT	check-in
ENREGISTREMENT ÉLECTRONIQUE	e-ticket check-in
PORTES DE DÉPART	departure gates

Checking In

Where's check-in?	**Où est l'enregistrement ?** *oo ay lawN•ruh• zhees•truh•mawN*
My name is…	**Je m'appelle…** *zhuh mah•pehl…*
I'm going to…	**Je vais à…** *zhuh vay ah…*
I have…	**J'ai…** *zhay…*
one suitcase	**une valise** *ewn vah•leez*
two suitcases	**deux valises** *duh vah•leez*
one piece of hand luggage	**un bagage à main** *uhN bah•gahzh ah mehN*
How much luggage is allowed?	**Combien de bagages sont permis ?** *kohN•beeyehN duh bah•gahzh sohN pehr•mee*

Is that pounds or kilos?	**Est-ce que ce sont des livres ou des kilos ?**
	ehs kuh suh sohN day leevr oo day kee·loh
Which terminal?	**Quel terminal ?** *kehl tehr·mee·nahl*
Which gate?	**Quelle porte ?** *kehl pohrt*
I'd like a window/aisle seat.	**Je voudrais un siège hublot/couloir.**
	zhuh an voo·dray uhN see·yehzh ew·bloh/kool·wahr
When do we leave/arrive ?	**Quand est-ce que nous partons/arrivons ?**
	kawN tehs kuh noo pahr·tohN/zah·ree·vohN
Is the flight delayed?	**Est-ce que le vol est retardé ?**
	ehs kuh luh vohl ay ruh·tahr·day
How late?	**Combien de retard a-t-il ?**
	kohN·beeyehN duh ruh·tahr ah·teel

YOU MAY HEAR...

Au suivant ! *oh swee·vawN*	Next!
Votre passeport/billet, s'il vous plaît.	Your passport/ticket,
voh·truh pahs·pohr/bee·yay seel voo play	please.
Avez-vous des bagages à enregistrer ?	Are you checking in
ah·vay·voo day bah·gahzh ah	any luggage?
awN·ruh·zhees·tray	
C'est trop gros pour un bagage à main.	That's too large for a
troh groh poor uhN bah·gahzh ah mehN	carry-on
	[piece of hand luggage].
Avez-vous fait ces bagages vous-même ?	Did you pack these
ah·vay·voo feh seh bah·gahzh voo·mehm	bags yourself?
Est-ce que quelqu'un vous a donné	Did anyone give you
quelque chose à porter ? *ehs kuh kehl·kuhN*	anything to carry?
voo zah doh·nay kehl·kuh shoh zah pohr·tay	

Retirer vos chaussures.   Take off your shoes.
ruh•tee•ray voh shoh•sewr

Embarquement immédiat...   Now boarding...
awN•bahr•kuh•mawN ee•meh•dyah...

Luggage

Where is/are...?	**Où est/sont...?** *oo ay/sohN...*
the luggage trolleys	**les chariots** *lay shah•ree•yoh*
the luggage lockers	**les consignes** *lay kohN•see•nyuh*
the baggage claim	**le retrait des bagages** *luh ruh•tray day bah•gahzh*
My luggage has been lost/stolen.	**Mon bagage a été perdu/volé.** *mohN bah•gahzh ah ay•tay pehr•dew/voh•lay*
My suitcase is damaged.	**Ma valise est endommagée.** *mah vah•leez ay awN•doh•mah•zhay*

Finding your Way

Where is/are...?	**Où est/sont...?** *oo ay/sohN...*
the currency exchange	**le bureau de change** *luh bew•roh duh shawNzh*
the car hire	**l'agence de voitures de location** *lah• zhawNs duh vwah•tewr duh loh•kah•seeyohN*
the exit	**la sortie** *lah sohr•tee*
the taxis	**les taxis** *lay tahk•see*
Is there... into town?	**Est-ce qu'il y a...pour aller en ville ?** *ehs keel•yah...poor ah•lay awN veel*
a bus	**un bus** *uhN bews*
a train	**un train** *uhN trehN*
a metro	**un métro** *uhN may•troh*

Train

Where's the train station?	**Où est la gare ?** *oo ay lah gahr*
How far is it?	**C'est loin d'ici ?** *say lwehN dee•see*
Where is/are...?	**Où est/sont...?** *oo ay/sohN...*
the ticket office	**le bureau de vente des billets** *luh bew•roh duh vawNt day bee•yay*
the information desk	**le bureau de renseignements** *luh bew•roh duh rawN•seh•nyuh•mawN*
the luggage lockers	**les consignes** *lay kohN•see•nyuh*
the platforms	**les quais** *lay kay*
Can I have a schedule [timetable]?	**Puis-je avoir les horaires ?** *pwee•zhuh ah•vwahr lay zhoh•rehr*
How long is the trip?	**Combien de temps dure le voyage ?** *kohN• beeyehN duh tawN dewr luh vwah•yahzh*
Is it a direct train?	**Est-ce que c'est un train direct ?** *ehs kuh say tuhN trehN dee•rehkt*
Do I have to change trains?	**Est-ce que je dois changer de train ?** *ehs kuh zhuh dwah shawN•zhay duh trehN*
Is the train on time?	**Est-ce que le train est à l'heure ?** *ehs kuh luh trehN ay aht luhr*

For Tickets, see page 18.

YOU MAY SEE...

QUAIS	platforms
INFORMATION	information
RÉSERVATIONS	reservations
SALLE D'ATTENTE	waiting room
ARRIVÉES	arrivals
DÉPARTS	departures

France has a fast and efficient train network operated by **SNCF** (**Société Nationale des Chemins de Fer**). The **SNCF** links over 50 cities in France, with the central hub in Paris. Paris has six train stations that service the rest of France and Europe. The **TGV** (**Train à Grande Vitesse**) is an extra-high-speed train that runs routes from Paris to Bordeaux, Brest, La Rochelle, Lille, Calais, Lyon and Marseille. Advance reservations are usually required.

The **Eurostar** offers fast and frequent service from London (St Pancras, or Ebbsfleet and Ashford in Kent) to Paris. The **Eurotunnel** provides car travel from Folkestone, U.K., to Calais, France.

Departures

Which track [platform] to...?	**Quel quai pour...?** *kehl kay poor...*
Is this the track [platform]/ train to...?	**Est-ce que c'est le quai/train pour...?** *ehs kuh say luh kay/trehN poor...*
Where is track [platform]...?	**Où est le quai...?** *oo ay luh kay...*
Where do I change for...?	**Où dois-je changer pour...?** *oo dwah•zhuh shawN•zhay poor...*

On Board

Can I sit here/open the window?	**Puis-je m'asseoir ici/ouvrir la fenêtre ?** *pwee•zhuh mah•swahr ee•see/oo•vreer lah fuh•neh•truh*
That's my seat.	**C'est ma place.** *say mah plahs*
Here's my reservation.	**Voici ma réservation.** *vwah•see mah ray•sehr•vah•seeyohN*

YOU MAY HEAR...

Billets, s'il vous plaît.   Tickets, please.
bee•yay seel voo play

Vous devez changer à...   You have to change at...
voo duh•vay shawN•zhay ah...

Prochain arrêt... *proh•shehN nah•reh...*   Next stop...

Bus

Where's the bus station?	**Où est la gare routière ?** *oo ay lah gahr roo-tee-yehr*
How far is it?	**C'est loin d'ici ?** *say lwehN dee•see*
How do I get to...?	**Comment vais-je à...?** *koh•mawN vay•zhuh ah...*
Is this the bus to...?	**Est-ce le bus pour...?** *ehs luh bews poor...*
Can you tell me when to get off?	**Pouvez-vous me dire quand je dois descendre ?** *poo•vay•voo muh deer kawN zhuh dwah deh•sawN•druh*
Do I have to change buses?	**Est-ce que je dois changer de bus ?** *ehs kuh zhuh dwah shawN•zhay duh bews*
Stop here, please!	**Arrêtez-vous ici, s'il vous plaît !** *ah•ray•tay•voo ee•see seel voo play*

For Tickets, see page 18.
For Asking Directions, see page 33.

Bus tickets can be purchased from the bus driver, or you can buy
them in metro stations or at tobacconists. Tickets purchased for the
metro can also be used for the bus system. Remember to validate your
ticket in the machine when boarding the bus.

YOU MAY SEE…

ARRÊT DE BUS	bus stop
DEMANDER L'ARRÊT	request stop
ENTRÉE/SORTIE	entrance/exit
COMPOSTER VOTRE BILLET	stamp your ticket

Metro

Where's the metro station?	**Où est la station de métro ?** *oo ay lah stah•seeyohN duh may•troh*
A map, please.	**Une carte, s'il vous plaît.** *ewn kahrt seel voo play*
Which line for…?	**Quelle est la ligne pour…?** *keh lay lah lee•nyuh poor…*
Which direction?	**Quelle direction ?** *kehl dee•rayk•seeyohN*
Do I have to transfer [change]?	**Est-ce que je dois changer de ligne ?** *ehs kuh zhuh dwah shawN•zhay duh lee•nyuh*
Is this the metro to…?	**Est-ce que c'est le métro pour…?** *ehs kuh say luh may•troh poor…*
How many stops to…?	**Combien d'arrêts jusqu'à…?** *kohN•beeyehN dah•ray zhew•skah…*

Where are we?	**Où sommes-nous ?** *oo suhm•noo*

For Tickets, see page 18.

Many of France's major cities have metro [subway] systems, including Paris, Lille, Toulouse, Lyon, Marseille, Rennes and Rouen. The metro systems are well marked with easy-to-read maps available at the stations. Most systems run from approximately 5:00 a.m. until 12:00 a.m., with some running slightly shorter or longer hours. In most cities, the same tickets work for the bus, metro and tram systems. Some cities require a ticket for each leg of the journey, while others allow you to travel the entire network on one ticket. Tickets can usually be purchased at the station or at tobacconists and other retailers.

Boat & Ferry

When is the ferry to…?	**Quand part le ferry pour…?** *kawN pahr luh fay•ree poor…*
Can I take my car?	**Est-ce que je peux prendre ma voiture ?** *ehs kuh zhuh puh prawN•druh mah vwah•tewr*
What time is the next sailing?	**À quelle heure est le prochain bateau ?** *ah kehl luhr ay luh proh•shehN bah•toh*
Can I book a seat/cabin?	**Puis-je réserver un siège/une cabine ?** *pwee•zhuh ray•zehr•vay uhN see•yehzh/ewn kah•been*
How long is the crossing?	**Combien de temps dure la traversée ?** *kohN•beeyehN duh tawN dewr lah trah•vehr•say*

For Tickets, see page 18.

YOU MAY SEE...

CANOTS DE SAUVETAGE	life boats
GILET DE SAUVETAGE	life jacket

Ferry service is available to and from the U.K., the Republic of Ireland and the Channel Islands to the north of France. Ferries carry cars as well as passengers. Services can be booked through the individual ferry companies or through a travel agent.

Taxi

Where can I get a taxi?	**Où puis-je prendre un taxi ?** *oo pwee-zhuh prawN-druh uhN tahk-see*
Can you send a taxi?	**Pouvez-vous envoyer un taxi ?** *poo-vay-voo awN-vwah-yay uhN tahk-see*
Do you have the number for a taxi?	**Avez-vous le numéro d'un taxi ?** *ah-vay-voo luh new-may-roh duhN tahk-see*
I'd like a taxi now/ for tomorrow at...	**Je voudrais un taxi maintenant/pour demain à...** *zhuh voo-dray uhN tahk-see mehN-tuh-nawN/poor duh-mehN ah...*
Pick me up at...	**Prenez-moi à...** *pruh-nay-mwah ah...*
I'm going to...	**Je vais à...** *zhuh vay zah...*
this address	**cette adresse** *seh tah-drehs*
the airport	**l'aéroport** *lah-ay-roh-pohr*
the train station	**la gare** *lah gahr*
I'm late.	**Je suis en retard.** *zhuh swee zawN ruh-tahr*
Can you drive faster/slower ?	**Pouvez-vous conduire plus/moins vite ?** *poo-vay-voo kohN-dweer plew/mwehN veet*

Stop/Wait here.	**Arrêtez/Attendez ici.**
	ah•ray•tay/ah•tawN•day ee•see
How much?	**Combien ça fait ?** *kohN•beeyehN sah fay*
You said it would cost…	**Vous aviez dit que cela coûterait…**
	voo zah•veeyay dee kuh suh•lah koo•tuh•ray…
Keep the change.	**Gardez la monnaie.** *gahr•day lah moh•nay*

YOU MAY HEAR…

Pour où ? *poor oo*
Quelle est l'adresse ? *keh lay lah•drehs*
Il y a une surcharge le soir/pour l'aéroport. *eel•yah ewn sewr•shahrzh luh swahr/poor lah•ay•roh•pohr*

Where to?
What's the address?
There's a nighttime/airport surcharge.

A taxi can be hailed on the street; available taxis can be spotted by the lit sign on the roof of the car. You can also wait for a taxi at stands, commonly located near train stations, metro stations and other tourist spots. Though tipping the driver isn't the norm, it's nice to do so for good service. There is usually a surcharge for each piece of luggage. The rate per kilometer may be different at night and for trips to the airport.

Bicycle & Motorbike

I'd like to hire…	**Je voudrais louer…** *zhuh voo·dray looway…*
a bicycle	**une bicyclette** *ewn bee·see·kleht*
a moped	**une mobylette** *ewn moh·bee·leht*
a motorcycle	**une moto** *ewn moh·toh*
How much per day/week?	**Combien par jour/semaine?** *kohN·beeyehN pahr zhoor/suh·mehn*
Can I have a helmet/lock?	**Puis-je avoir un casque/cadenas?** *pwee·zhuh ah·vwahr uhN kas·kuh/kah·duh·nah*

Car Hire

Where's the car hire?	**Où est l'agence de location de voitures?** *oo ay lah·zhawNs duh loh·kah·seeyohN duh vwah·tewr*
I'd like…	**Je voudrais…** *zhuh voo·dray…*
a cheap/small car	**une voiture bon marché/petite voiture** *ewn vwah·tewr bohN mahr·shay/puh·teet vwah·tewr*
an automatic/ a manual	**une automatique/manuelle** *ewn oh·toh·mah·teek/mah·new·ehl*
air conditioning	**la climatisation** *lah klee·mah·tee·zah·seeyohN*
a car seat	**un siège bébé** *uhN seeyehzh bay·bay*
How much…?	**Combien ça coûte…?** *kohN·beeyehN sah koot…*
per day/week	**par jour/semaine** *pahr zhoor/suh·mehN*
per kilometer	**par kilomètre** *pahr kee·loh·meh·truh*
for unlimited mileage	**pour un kilométrage illimité** *poor uhN kee·loh·meh·trahzh ee·lee·mee·tay*
with insurance	**avec assurance** *ah·vehk ah·sew·rawNs*
Are there any discounts?	**Y-a-t-il des réductions?** *yah·teel day ray·dewk·seeyohN*

YOU MAY HEAR...

Avez-vous un permis de conduire international ? *ah•vay•voo uhN pehr•mee duh kohN•dweer ehN•tehr•nah•seeyoh•nahl*

Do you have an international driver's license?

Votre passeport, s'il vous plaît. *voh•truh pahs•pohr seel voo play*

Your passport, please.

Voulez-vous prendre une assurance ? *Voo•lay•voo prawN•druh ewn ah•sew•rawNs*

Do you want insurance?

J'ai besoin d'un acompte. *zhay buh•zwehN duhN ah•kohNt*

I'll need a deposit.

Vos initiales/Signez ici. *voh zee•nee•seeyahl/see•nyay zee•see*

Initial/Sign here.

Fuel Station

Where's the fuel station?	**Où est la station service ?** *oo ay lah stah• seeyohN sehr•vees*
Fill it up.	**Faites-le plein.** *feht•luh plehN*
...euros, please.	**...euros, s'il vous plaît.** *...uh•roh seel voo play*
I'll pay in cash/by credit card.	**Je paierai en espèces/par carte de crédit.** *zhuh pay•ray awN nehs•pehs/pahr kahrt duh kray•dee*

For Numbers, see page 173.

YOU MAY SEE...

ESSENCE	gas [petrol]
SANS PLOMB	unleaded
ORDINAIRE	regular
SUPER	super
GAZOLE	diesel

Asking Directions

Is this the way to…?	**Est-ce le chemin pour…?**
	ehs luh shuh·mehN poor…
How far is it to…?	**À quelle distance se trouve…?**
	ah kehl dees·tawNs suh troov…
Where's…?	**Où est…?** *oo ay…*
…Street	**la rue…** *lah rew…*
this address	**cette adresse** *seh tah·drehs*
the highway [motorway]	**l'autoroute** *loh·toh·root*
Can you show me on the map?	**Pouvez-vous me montrer sur la carte ?**
	poo·vay·voo muh mohN·tray sewr lah kahrt
I'm lost.	**Je suis perdu m /perdue f.**
	zhuh swee pehr·dew

YOU MAY HEAR…

tout droit *too drwah*	straight ahead
à gauche *ah gohsh*	left
à droite *ah drwaht*	right
au coin *oh kwehN*	around the corner
à l'opposé *ah loh·poh·zay*	opposite
derrière *deh·reeyehr*	behind
près de *pray duh*	next to
après *ah·pray*	after
nord/sud *nohr/sewd*	north/south
est/ouest *ehst/oowehst*	east/west
au feu (tricolore) *oh fuh (tree·koh·lohr)*	at the traffic light
au carrefour *oh cahr·foor*	at the intersection

YOU MAY SEE...

STOP	**STOP**	stop
	CÉDEZ LE PASSAGE	yield
	STATIONNEMENT INTERDIT	no parking
	SENS UNIQUE	one way
	SENS INTERDIT	no entry
	CIRCULATION INTERDITE	no vehicles allowed
	INTERDICTION DE DÉPASSER	no passing
	FEU TRICOLORE	traffic signal ahead
	SORTIE	exit

Parking

Can I park here?	**Puis-je me garer ici ?** pwee-zhuh muh gah-ray ee-see
Where's...?	**Où est...?** oo ay...
the parking garage	**le garage** luh gah-rahzh
the parking lot [car park]	**le parking** luh pahr-keeng
the parking meter	**l'horodateur** loh-roh-dah-tuhr
How much...?	**Combien ça coûte...?** kohN-beeyehN sah koot...

per hour	**par heure** *pahr uhr*
per day	**par jour** *pahr zhoor*
for overnight	**toute la nuit** *toot lah nwee*

Parking in larger cities is sometimes hard to find. Parking on the street is possible; you'll usually have to purchase a ticket from a machine for a certain length of time and display it in your windshield. Parking is not allowed on red marked areas or near yellow-marked curbs. Parking garages can be found in downtown areas, though their rates can be expensive.

Breakdown & Repair

My car broke down/ won't start.	**Ma voiture est tombée en panne/ne démarre pas.** *mah vwah·tewr ay tohN·bay awN pahn/nuh day·mahr pah*
Can you fix it (today)?	**Pouvez-vous la réparer (aujourd'hui) ?** *poo·vay·voo lah ray·pah·ray (oh·zhoor·dwee)*
When will it be ready?	**Quand cela sera-t-il prêt ?** *kawN suh·lah suh·rah·teel pray*
How much?	**Combien ça coûte ?** *kohN·beeyehN sah koot*
I have a puncture/ flat tyre (tire)	**J'ai un pneu crevé/Mon pneu est crevé** *zhay uhN pnuh kruh·vay / mohN pnuh ay kruh·vay*

Accidents

| There was an accident. | **Il y a eu un accident.** *eel·yah ew uhN nahk· see·dawN* |
| Call an ambulance/ the police. | **Appelez une ambulance/la police.** *ah·puh·lay ewn nawN·bew·lawNs/lah poh·lees* |

Places to Stay

ESSENTIAL

Can you recommend a hotel?	**Pouvez-vous me conseiller un hôtel ?** *poo·vay·voo muh kohN·say·yay uhN noh·tehl*
I made a reservation.	**J'ai fait une réservation.** *zhay fay ewn ray·zehr·vah·seeyohN*
My name is…	**Mon nom est…** *mohN nohN ay…*
Do you have a room…?	**Avez-vous une chambre…?** *ah·vay·voo ewn shawN·bruh…*
for one/two	**pour un/deux** *poor uhN/duh*
with a bathroom	**avec salle de bains** *ah·vehk sahl duh behN*
with air conditioning	**avec climatisation** *ah·vehk klee·mah·tee·zah·seeyohN*
For…	**Pour…** *poor…*
tonight	**ce soir** *suh swahr*
two nights	**deux nuits** *duh nwee*
one week	**une semaine** *ewn suh·mehn*
How much?	**Combien ça coûte ?** *kohN·beeyehN sah koot*
Is there anything cheaper?	**N'y-a-t-il rien de moins cher ?** *Nee·yah·teel reeyehN duh mwehN shehr*
When's check-out?	**Quand dois-je quitter la chambre ?** *kawN dwah·zhuh kee·tay lah shawN·bruh*
Can I leave this in the safe?	**Puis-je laisser ceci dans le coffre ?** *pwee·zhuh lay·say suh·see dawN luh koh·fruh*
Can I leave my bags?	**Puis-je laisser mes bagages ?** *pwee·zhuh lay·say meh bah·gahzh*
Can I have my bill/ a receipt ?	**Puis-je avoir ma facture/un reçu ?** *pwee·zhuh ah·vwahr mah fahk·tewr/uhN ruh·sew*
I'll pay in cash/by credit card.	**Je paierai en espèces/par carte de crédit.** *zhuh pay·ray awN nehs·pehs/pahr kahrt duh kray·dee*

If you didn't reserve accommodations before your trip, visit the local **Office de Tourisme** (Tourist Information Office) for recommendations on places to stay.

Somewhere to Stay

Can you recommend...?	**Pouvez-vous me conseiller...?** *poo·vay·voo muh kohN·say·yay...*
a hotel	**un hôtel** *uhN noh·tehl*
a hostel	**une auberge de jeunesse** *ewn oh·behrzh duh zhuh·nehs*
a campsite	**un camping** *uhN kawN·peeng*
a bed and breakfast	**un bed and breakfast** *uhN behd ahnd brayk·fahst*
What is it near?	**C'est près de quoi ?** *say pray duh kwah*
How do I get there?	**Comment est-ce que je m'y rends ?** *koh·mawN ehs kuh zhuh mee rawN*

Hotels in France are ranked in categories or stars; the higher the category or number of stars, the more luxurious and expensive the hotel. **Relais** and **châteaux** are former castles, monasteries, manor houses or abbeys that have been converted into high-end accommodations. **Gîtes-chambres d'hôte** are rentable guestrooms, usually in a village home or on a farm, sometimes referred to as agritourism. Condos, apartments and villas are available for those with larger groups or families or who are staying in one place for at least a week. Hostels and campsites are also available.

At the Hotel

I have a reservation.	**J'ai une réservation.**
	zhay ewn ray·zehr·vah·seeyohN
My name is...	**Mon nom est...** *mohN nohN may...*
Do you have	**Avez-vous une chambre...?**
a room...?	*ah·vay·voo ewn shawN·bruh...*
with a	**avec toilettes/douche**
toilet/shower	*ah·vehk twah·leht/doosh*
with air conditioning	**climatisée** *klee·mah·tee·zay*
that's smoking/	**fumeur/non-fumeur**
non-smoking	*few·muhr/ nohN·few·muhr*
For...	**Pour...** *poor...*
tonight	**ce soir** *suh swahr*
two nights	**deux nuits** *duh nwee*
a week	**une semaine** *ewn suh·mehn*
Do you have...?	**Avez-vous...?** *ah·vay·voo...*
a computer	**un ordinateur** *uhN nohr·dee·nah·tuhr*
an elevator [a lift]	**un ascenseur** *uhN nah·sawN·suhr*
(wireless) internet	**une connexion internet (Wi-Fi)**
service	*ewn koh·nek·seeyohN ehN·tehr·neht (wee·fee)*
room service	**un service de chambres**
	uhN sehr·vees duh shawN·bruh
a pool	**une piscine** *ewn pee·seen*
a gym	**une salle de gym** *ewn sahl duh zheem*
I need...	**J'ai besoin...** *zhay buh·zwehN...*
an extra bed	**d'un lit supplémentaire**
	duhN lee sew·play·mawN·tehr
a cot	**d'un lit pliant** *duhN lee plee·yawN*
a crib	**d'un berceau** *duhN behr·soh*

For Numbers, see page 173.

YOU MAY HEAR...

Votre passeport/carte de crédit, s'il vous plaît. *voh•truh pahs•pohr/kahrt duh kray•dee seel voo play*

Your passport/credit card, please.

Remplissez cette fiche. *rawN•plee•say seht feesh*

Fill out this form.

Signez ici. *see•nyay ee•see*

Sign here.

Price

How much per night/week?	**Quel est le tarif par nuit/semaine ?** *kehl eh luh tah-reef pahr nwee/suh•mehn*
Does that include breakfast/tax?	**Est-ce que cela comprend le petit déjeuner/la TVA ?** *ehs kuh suh•lah kohN•prawN luh puh•tee day•zhuh•nay/lah tay•vay•ah*
Are there any discounts?	**Y-a-t-il des réductions ?** *yah•teel deh ray•dewk•seeyohN*

Preferences

Can I see the room?	**Puis-je voir la chambre ?**
	pwee·zhuh vwahr lah shawN·bruh
I'd like a…room.	**Je voudrais une chambre…**
	zhuh voo·dray ewn shawN·bruh…
better	**plus confortable** *plew kohN·fohr·tah·bluh*
bigger	**plus grande** *plew grawNd*
cheaper	**moins chère** *mwehN shehr*
quieter	**plus calme** *plew kahlm*
I'll take it.	**Je la prends.** *zhuh lah prawN*
No, I won't take it.	**Non, je ne la prends pas.**
	nohN zhuh nuh lah prawN pah

Questions

Where is/are…?	**Où est/sont…?** *oo ay/sohN…*
the bar	**le bar** *luh bahr*
the bathrooms	**les toilettes** *lay twah·leht*
the elevator [lift]	**l'ascenseur** *lah·sawN·suhr*
I'd like…	**Je voudrais…** *zhuh voo·dray…*
a blanket	**une couverture** *ewn koo·vehr·tewr*
an iron	**un fer à repasser** *uhN feh rah ruh·pah·say*
the room	**la clé/carte de la chambre**
key/key card	*lah klay/kahrt duh lah shawN·bruh*
a pillow	**un oreiller** *uhN noh·reh·yay*
soap	**du savon** *dew sah·vohN*
toilet paper	**du papier toilette** *dew pah·pee·yay twah·leht*
a towel	**une serviette** *ewn sehr·veeyeht*
Do you have an	**Avez-vous un adaptateur pour ceci ?**
adapter for this?	*ah·vay·voo uhN nah·dahp·tah·tuhr poor suh·see*
How do you turn	**Comment allume-t-on les lumières ?**

on the lights?	*koh•mawN ah•lewm•tohN lay lew•mee•yehr*
Can you wake me at...?	**Pouvez-vous me réveiller à...?** *poo•vay•voo muh ray•veh•yay ah...*
Can I leave this in the safe?	**Puis-je laisser ceci dans le coffre ?** *pwee•zhuh lay•say suh•see dawN luh koh•fruh*
Can I have my things from the safe?	**Puis-je prendre mes affaires qui sont dans le coffre?** *pwee•zhuh prawN•druh meh zah•fehr kee sohN dawN luh koh•fruh*
Is there mail/ a message for me?	**Y-a-t-il du courrier/un message pour moi ?** *yah•teel dew koo•reeyay/uhN meh•sahzh poor mwah*
Do you have a laundry service?	**Avez-vous un service de blanchisserie ?** *ah•vay•voo uhN sehr•vees duh blawN•shee•suh•ree*

YOU MAY SEE...

POUSSER/TIRER	push/pull
TOILETTES	bathroom [toilet]
DOUCHES	showers
ASCENSEUR	elevator [lift]
ESCALIERS	stairs
DISTRIBUTEURS	vending machines
GLACE	ice
TEINTURERIE	laundry
NE PAS DÉRANGER	do not disturb
PORTE COUPE-FEU	fire door
SORTIE (DE SECOURS)	(emergency) exit
APPEL RÉVEIL	wake-up call

Problems

There's a problem.	**Il y a un problème.**	*eel·yah uhN proh·blehm*
I lost my key/key card.	**J'ai perdu la clé/carte de ma chambre.**	*zhay pehr·dew lah klay/kahrt duh mah shawN·bruh*
I've locked my key/key card in the room.	**J'ai laissé ma clé/carte à l'intérieur de ma chambre.**	*zhay leh·say mah klay/kahrt ah lehN·tay·reeyuhr duh mah shawN·bruh*
There's no hot water/toilet paper.	**Il n'y a pas d'eau chaude/de papier toilette.**	*eel nee·yah pah doh shohd/duh pah·pee·yay twah·leht*
The room is dirty.	**La chambre est sale.**	*lah shawN·bruh ay sahl*
There are bugs in the room.	**Il y a des insectes dans la chambre.**	*eel·yah day zehN·sehkt dawN lah shawN·bruh*
...doesn't work.	**...ne fonctionne pas.**	*...nuh fohNk·seeyohn pah*
Can you fix...?	**Pouvez-vous réparer...?**	*poo·vay·voo ray·pah·ray...*
the air conditioning	**la climatisation**	*lah klee·mah·tee·zah·seeyohN*
the fan	**le ventilateur**	*luh vawN·tee·lah·tuhr*

the heat [heating]	**le chauffage** *luh shoh•fahzh*
the light	**la lumière** *lah lew•mee•yehr*
the TV	**la télé** *lah tay•lay*
the toilet	**les toilettes** *lay twah•leht*
I'd like another room	**Je voudrais une autre chambre.**
	zhuh voo•dray zewn oh•truh shawN•bruh

Unlike the U.S., most of Europe runs on 220-volt electricity, and plugs are two-pronged. You may need a converter and/or an adapter for your appliance.

Checking Out

When's check-out?	**Quand dois-je quitter la chambre ?**
	kawN dwah•zhuh kee•tay lah shawN•bruh
Can I leave my bags here until…?	**Puis-je laisser mes bagages ici jusqu'à…?**
	pwee•zhuh leh•say meh bah•gahzh ee•see zhew•skah…
Can I have an itemized bill/ a receipt ?	**Puis-je avoir une facture détaillée/un reçu ?**
	pwee•zhuh ah•vwahr ewn fahk•tewr day•tie•yay/uhN ruh•sew
I think there's a mistake.	**Je pense qu'il y a une erreur.**
	zhuh pawNs keel•yah ewn ay•ruhr
I'll pay in cash/by credit card.	**Je paierai en espèces/par carte de crédit.**
	zhuh pay•ray awN nehs•pehs/pahr kahrt duh kray•dee

It is customary to give a tip to porters, hotel bartenders, room service staff and maids; however, this is not a set rule so ask at the reception desk. You should tip the porter €1-1.50 per piece of luggage. A tip of €1.50 per day is adequate for maid service. Room service employees and bartenders can be tipped an extra €0.50-1 if service was good; the customary tip amount is already included in the total of your bill.

Renting

I reserved an apartment/a room.	**J'ai réservé un appartement/une chambre.** *zhay ray·zehr·vay uhN nah·pahrt·mawN/ewn shawN·bruh*
My name is...	**Je m'appelle...** *zhuh mah·pehl...*
Can I have the keys?	**Puis-je avoir les clés ?** *pwee·zhuh ah·vwahr lay klay*
Are there...?	**Y-a-t-il des...?** *yah·teel day...*
dishes	**assiettes** *ah·seeyeht*
pillows	**oreillers** *oh·reh·yay*
sheets	**draps** *drah*
towels	**serviettes** *sehr·veeyeht*
kitchen utensils	**ustensiles de cuisine** *ews·tawN·seel duh kwee·zeen*
When do I put out the bins/recycling ?	**Quand dois-je sortir les poubelles/ordures à recycler ?** *kawN dwah·zhuh sohr·teer lay poo·behl/zohr·dewr ah ruh·seek·lay*
...is broken.	**...est cassé m /cassée f.** *...ay kah·say*
How does... work?	**Comment fonctionne...?** *koh·mawN fohNk·seeyohn...*
the air conditioner	**la climatisation** *lah klee·mah·tee·zah·seeyohN*

the dishwasher	**le lave-vaisselle** *luh lahv·veh·sehl*
the freezer	**le congélateur** *luh kohN·zhay·lah·tuhr*
the heater	**le chauffage** *luh shoh·fahzh*
the microwave	**le micro-onde** *luh mee·kroh·ohNd*
the refrigerator	**le réfrigérateur** *luh ray·free·zhay·rah·tuhr*
the stove	**la gazinière** *lah gah·zee·neeyehr*
the washing machine	**la machine à laver** *lah mah·sheen ah lah·vay*

Domestic Items

I need...	**J'ai besoin...** *zhay buh·zwehN...*
an adapter	**d'un adaptateur** *duhN nah·dahp·tah·tuhr*
aluminum [foil]	**de papier aluminium** *duh pah·peeyay ah·lew·mee·neeyewm*
a bottle opener	**d'un ouvre-bouteille** *duhN oo·vruh·boo·tehy*
a broom	**d'un balai** *duhN bah·lay*
a can opener	**d'un ouvre boîte** *duhN noo·vruh bwaht*
cleaning supplies	**de produits d'entretien** *duh proh·dwee dawN·truh·teeyehN*
a corkscrew	**d'un tire-bouchon** *duhN teer·boo·shohN*
detergent	**de détergent** *duh day·tehr·zhawN*
dishwashing liquid	**de détergent pour lave-vaisselle** *duh day·tehr·zhawN poor lahv·veh·sehl*
bin bags	**de sacs poubelles** *duh sahk poo·behl*
a lightbulb	**d'une ampoule** *dewn nawN·pool*
matches	**d'allumettes** *dah·lew·meht*
a mop	**d'une serpillière** *dewn sehr·peeyehr*
napkins	**de serviettes de table** *duh sehr·veeyeht duh tah·bluh*
paper towels	**de serviettes en papier** *duh sehr·veeyeht awN pah·peeyay*

plastic wrap [cling film]	**de cellophane** *duh seh·loh·fahn*
a plunger	**d'un déboucheur de toilettes**
	duhN day·boo·shur duh twah·leht
scissors	**de ciseaux** *duh see·zoh*
a vacuum cleaner	**d'un aspirateur** *duhN nah·spee·rah·tuhr*

For In the Kitchen, see page 83.

At the Hostel

Is there a bed available?	**Y-a-t-il un lit de libre ?** *yah·teel uhN lee duh lee·bruh*
I'd like...	**Je voudrais...** *zhuh voo·dray...*
a single/double room	**une chambre simple/double** *ewn shawN·bruh sehN·pluh/doo·bluh*
a blanket	**une couverture** *ewn koo·vehr·tewr*
a pillow	**un oreiller** *uhN noh·reh·yay*
sheets	**des draps** *day drah*
a towel	**une serviette de bain** *ewn sehr·veeyeht duh behN*
Do you have lockers?	**Avez-vous des cadenas ?** *ah·vay·voo day cah·duh·nah*
When do you up?	**Quand fermez-vous ?** *kawN fehr·may·voo lock*
Do I need a membership card?	**Ai-je besoin d'une carte de membre ?** *ay·zhuh buh·zwehN dewn kahrt duh mawN·bruh*
Here's my international student card.	**Voici ma carte internationale d'étudiant.** *vwah·see mah kahrt ehN·tehr·nah·seeyoh·nahl day·tew·deeyawN*

Present your accredited Youth Hostel Association card to stay in a French hostel run by the **Fédération Unie des Auberges de Jeunesse (FUAJ)** or the **Ligue Française pour les Auberges de Jeunesse (LFAJ)**. **Gîtes d'Étapes** offer hostel accommodation that is popular with hikers, usually in or near national parks; no membership is needed. Hostels fill up quickly during tourist seasons; make reservations well in advance. Many hostels accept online reservations.

Going Camping

Can I camp here?	**Puis-je camper ici ?**
	pwee·zhuh kawN·pay ee·see
Where's the campsite?	**Où est le camping ?** *oo ay luh kawN·peeng*
What is the charge per day/week?	**Quel est le prix par jour/semaine ?**
	keh lay luh pree pahr zhoor/suh·mehn
Are there...?	**Y-a-t-il...?** *yah·teel...*
cooking facilities	**des cuisines** *day kwee·zeen*
electric outlets	**des prises électriques**
	day pree zay·lehk·treek

laundry facilities	**des buanderies** *day bew•awN•dree*
showers	**des douches** *day doosh*
tents for hire	**des tentes à louer** *day tawN tah looway*
Where can I empty the chemical toilet?	**Où puis-je vider les toilettes portables ?** *oo pwee•zhuh vee•day lay twah•leht pohr•tah•bluh*

YOU MAY SEE...

EAU POTABLE	drinking water
CAMPING INTERDIT	no camping
FEUX DE BOIS/BARBECUES INTERDITS	no fires/barbecues

For Domestic Items, see page 45.
For In the Kitchen, see page 83.

Communications

ESSENTIAL

Where's an internet cafe?	**Où y-a-t-il un cyber café ?** *oo yah•teel uhN see•behr kah•fay*
Can I access the internet/check my e-mail ?	**Puis-je me connecter à Internet/consulter mes mails ?** *pwee•zhuh muh koh•nehk•tay ah ehN•tehr•neht/kohN•sewl•tay may mehyl*
How much per half hour/hour?	**Combien coûte la demi-heure/l'heure ?** *kohN•beeyehN koot lah duh•mee•uhr/luhr*
How do I	**Comment est-ce que je me connecte/**

connect/log on?	**j'ouvre une session ?** *koh·mawN ehs kuh zhuh muh koh·nehkt/zhoo·vruh ewn seh·seeyohN*
A phone card, please.	**Une carte de téléphone, s'il vous plaît.** *ewn kahrt duh tay·lay·fohn seel voo play*
Can I have your phone number?	**Puis-je avoir votre numéro de téléphone ?** *pwee·zhuh ah·vwahr voh·truh new·meh·roh duh tay·lay·fohn*
Here's my number/e-mail.	**Voici mon numéro/mail.** *vwah·see mohN new·meh·roh/mehyl*
Call me.	**Appelle-moi.** *ah·pehl·mwah*
E-mail me.	**Envoie-moi un mail.** *awN·vwah·mwah uhN mehyl*
Hello. This is…	**Bonjour. C'est…** *bohN·zhoor say…*
Can I speak to…?	**Puis-je parler à…?** *pwee·zhuh pahr·lay ah…*
Can you repeat that?	**Pouvez-vous répéter cela ?** *poo·vay·voo ray·pay·tay suh·lah*
I'll call back later.	**Je rappellerai plus tard.** *zhuh rah·peh·luh·ray plew tahr*
Bye.	**Au revoir.** *oh ruh·vwahr*
Where's the post office?	**Où est la poste ?** *oo ay lah pohst*
I'd like to send this to…	**Je voudrais envoyer ceci à…** *zhuh voo·dray zawN·vwah·yay suh·see ah…*

French language purists prefer to avoid using words adopted directly from English, but their best efforts can't always change popular usage. Even though you may see and hear the official dictionary-approved word for e-mail, **courriel** (short for **courrier-électronique**, electronic mail), the word **mail** is the one most often used in France and what you will see used throughout this book.

Online

Where's an internet cafe?	**Où y-a-t-il un cyber café ?** *oo yah•teel uhN see•behr kah•fay*
Does it have wireless internet?	**Est-ce qu'il a la connexion Wi-Fi ?** *ehs kee•lee ah lah koh•nehk•seeyohN wee•fee*
What is the WiFi password?	**Quel est le mot de passe du WiFi ?** *keh lay luh moh duh pahs dew wee•fee*
Is the WiFi free?	**Est-ce que le WiFi est gratuit ?** *ehs kuh luh wee•fee ay grah•twee*
Do you have bluetooth?	**Avez-vous Bluetooth ?** *ah•vay•voo bloo•toohs*
Can you show me how to turn on/off the computer?	**Pouvez-vous me montrer comment allumer/éteindre l'ordinateur ?** *poo•vay•voo muh mohN•tray koh•mawN ah•lew•may/eh•tehyuhn•druh lohr•dee•nah•tuhr*
Can I...?	**Puis-je...?** *pwee•zhuh...*
access the internet	**accéder à Internet** *ahk•seh•day ah ehN•tehrneht*
check my email	**consulter mes mails** *kohN•sewl•tay may mehyl*
print	**imprimer** *ehN•pree•may*
plug in/charge my	**brancher/charger mon ordinateur portable/**

laptop/iPhone/ iPad/BlackBerry?	**iPhone/iPad/Blackberry ?** *brawN•shay/ shahr•zhay mohN nohr•dee•nah•tuhr pohr•tah•bluh / ee•fohn / ee•pahd / black•ber•ee*
access Skype?	**accéder à Skype ?** *ah•ksay•day ah skiep*
How much per half hour/hour?	**Combien coûte la demi-heure/l'heure ?** *kohN•beeyehN koot lah duh•mee•uhr/luhr*
How do I…?	**Comment est-ce que…?** *koh•mawN ehs kuh…*
connect/disconnect	**je me connecte/déconnecte** *zhuh muh koh•nehkt/day•koh•nehkt*
log on/off	**j'ouvre/je termine la session** *zhoo•vruh/zhuh tehr•meen lah seh•seeyohN*
type this symbol	**je frappe ce symbole** *zhuh frahp suh sehN•bohl*
What's your email?	**Quel est votre mail ?** *keh lay voh•truh mehyl*
My email is…	**Mon mail est…** *mohN mehyl ay…*
Do you have a scanner?	**Avez-vous un scanneur ?** *ah•vay•voo uhN skah•nuhr*

Social Media

Are you on Facebook/Twitter?	**Etes-vous sur Facebook/Twitter ?** (polite form) *eht•voo sewr fayhs•book/twee•teuhr*
	Es-tu sur Facebook/Twitter ? (informal form) *eh•tew sewr fayhs•book/twee•teuhr*
What's your user name?	**Quel est votre nom d'utilisateur ?** (polite form) *keh lay voh•truh nohN dew•tee•lee•zah•tuhr*
	Quel est ton nom d'utilisateur ? (informal form) *keh lay tohN nohN dew•tee•lee•zah•tuhr*
I'll add you as a friend.	**Je vous ajouterai comme ami.** (polite form) *zhuh voo zah•zhoo•tray kohm ah•mee*
	Je t'ajouterai comme ami. (informal form) *zhuh tah•zhoo•tray kohm ah•mee*

I'll follow you on Twitter. **Je vous suivrai sur Twitter.** (polite form)

zhuh voo swee•vray sewr twitter

Je te suivrai sur Twitter. (informal form)

zhuh tuh swee•vray sewr twitter

Are you following...? **Suivez-vous...?** (polite form) *swee•vay voo*

Suis-tu...? (informal form) *swee tew*

I'll put the pictures on Facebook/Twitter. **Je mettrai les photos sur Facebook/Twitter.**

zhuh may•tray lay foh•toh sewr fayhs•book/ twee•teuhr

I'll tag you in the pictures. **Je vous marquerai sur les photos.** (polite form)

zhuh voo mahr•kuh•ray sewr lay foh•toh

Je te marquerai sur les photos. (informal form)

zhuh tuh mahr•kuh•ray sewr lay foh•toh

YOU MAY SEE...

FERMER	close
SUPPRIMER	delete
MAIL	e-mail
SORTIR	exit
AIDE	help
MESSAGERIE INSTANTANÉE	instant messenger
INTERNET	internet
OUVRIR UNE SESSION	log in
NOUVEAU (MESSAGE)	new (message)
ALLUMÉ/ÉTEINT	on/off
OUVRIR	open
IMPRIMER	print
SAUVEGARDER	save
ENVOYER	send

Phone

A phone card/ prepaid phone, please.	**Une carte de téléphone/téléphone prépayé, s'il vous plaît.** *ewn kahrt duh tay•lay•fohn/tay•lay•fohn pray•pay•yay seel voo play*
How much?	**Combien ça coûte?** *kohN•beeyehN sah koot*
Where's the pay phone?	**Où y-a-t-il une cabine téléphonique?** *oo yah•teel ewn kah•been tay•lay•foh•neek*
What's the area/ country code for…?	**Quel est le code régional/national pour…?** *keh lay luh kohd ray•zheeyoh•nahl/ nah•seeyoh•nahl poor…*
What's the number for Information?	**Quel est le numéro des renseignements?** *keh lay luh new•may•roh day rawN•seh•nyuh•mawN*
I'd like the number for…	**Puis-je avoir le numéro de…** *pwee•zhuh ah•vwahr luh new•may•roh duh…*
I'd like to call collect [reverse the charges].	**Je voudrais appeler en PCV.** *zhuh voo•dray zah•puh•lay awN pay•say•vay*
My phone doesn't work here.	**Mon téléphone est en panne.** *mohN tay•lay•fohn ayt awN pahn*
What network are you on?	**Quel réseau utilisez-vous?** *kehl ray•zoh ew•tee•lee•zay voo*
Is it 3G?	**Est-ce que c'est un réseau 3G?** *ehs kuh say uhN ray•zoh trwah zhay*

I have run out of credit/minutes.	**J'ai épuisé mon crédit/mes minutes.** *zhay ay•pwee•zay mohN kray•dee/meh mee•newt*
Can I buy some credit?	**Puis-je acheter du crédit ?** *pwee•zhuh ah•shtay dew kray•dee*
Do you have a phone charger?	**Avez-vous un chargeur pour téléphone ?** *ah•vay•voo uhN shahr•zhuhr poor tay•lay•fohn*
Can I have your number?	**Puis-je avoir votre numéro ?** *pwee•zhuh ah•vwahr voh•truh new•meh•roh*
Here's my number.	**Voici mon numéro.** *vwah•see mohN new•may•roh*
Please call/text me.	**S'il vous plaît, appelez-moi/envoyez-moi un SMS.** *seel voo play ah•puh•lay•mwah/ awN•vwah•yay•mwah uhN ehs•ehm•ehs*
I'll call/text you.	**Je vous appellerai/enverrai un SMS.** *zhuh voo zah•peh•luh•ray/zawN•veh•ray uhN nehs•ehm•ehs*

For Numbers, see page 173.

Telephone Etiquette

Hello. This is...	**Bonjour. C'est...** *bohN•zhoor say...*
Can I speak to...?	**Puis-je parler à...?** *pwee•zhuh pahr•lay ah...*
Extension...	**Poste...** *pohst...*
Speak louder/more slowly, please.	**Parlez plus fort/lentement, s'il vous plaît.** *pahr•lay plew fohr/lawN•tuh•mawN seel voo play*
Can you repeat that?	**Pouvez-vous répéter cela ?** *poo•vay•voo ray•pay•tay suh•lah*
I'll call back later.	**Je rappellerai plus tard.** *zhuh rah•peh•luh•ray plew tahr*
Bye.	**Au revoir.** *oh ruh•vwahr*

YOU MAY HEAR...

Qui est à l'appareil ?
kee ay aht lah•pah•rehy

Who's calling?

Attendez un instant.
ah•tawN•day uhN nehN•stawN

Hold on.

Je vous le *m* /la *f* passe.
zhuh voo luh /lah pahs

I'll put you through to him/her.

Il *m* /Elle *f* n'est pas là/est sur une autre ligne.
Eel /ehl nay pah lah/ay sewr ewn oh•truh lee•nyuh

He/She is not here/on another line.

Voulez-vous laisser un message ?
voo•lay•voo leh•say uhN meh•sahzh

Would you like to leave a message?

Rappelez plus tard/dans dix minutes.
rah•puh•lay plew tahr/dawN dee mee•newt

Call back later/in ten minutes.

Peut-il *m* /Peut-elle *f* vous rappeler ?
puh•teel /puh•tehl voo rah•puh•lay

Can he/she call you back?

Quel est votre numéro de téléphone ?
keh lay voh•truh new•may•roh duh tay•lay•fohn

What's your number?

Most pay phones in France are card operated; some require phone cards, others, credit cards. You can purchase phone cards at **tabacs** (tobacconists), at **la Poste** (the post office) and wherever you see the sign **Télécarte**. French phone numbers have 10 digits, including a two digit regional prefix. When calling within the country, you must dial all 10 digits, even when dialing within the same region. When dialing from outside the country, delete the first 0 (part of the regional prefix). To call the U.S. or Canada from France, dial 001 + area code + phone number. To call the U.K. from France, dial 0044 + area code (minus the first 0) + phone number.

Fax

Can I send/receive a fax here?	**Puis-je envoyer/recevoir un fax ici ?** *pwee·zhuh awN·vwah·yay/ruh·suh·vwah ruhN fahks ee·see*
What's the fax number?	**Quel est le numéro de fax ?** *keh lay luh new·may·roh duh fahks*
Please fax this to...	**S'il vous plaît, faxer ceci au...** *seel voo play fahk·say suh·see oh...*

Post

Where's the post office/mailbox?	**Où est la poste/boîte aux lettres ?** *oo ay lah pohst/bwah·toh·leh·truh*
A stamp for this postcard/letter to...	**Un timbre pour cette carte postale/lettre pour...** *uhN tehN·bruh poor seht kahrt pohs·tahl/leh·truh poor...*
How much?	**Combien ça coûte ?** *kohN·beeyehN sah koot*

Send this package by airmail/express.	**Envoyez ce paquet par avion/en express.**
	awN•vwah•yay suh pah•keh pah rah•veeyohN/ awN ehk•sprehs
A receipt, please.	**Un reçu, s'il vous plaît.**
	uhN ruh•sew seel voo play

YOU MAY HEAR...

Remplissez ce formulaire de déclaration de douane.	Fill out the customs declaration form.
rawN•plee•say suh fohr•mew•lehr duh day•klah•rah•seeyohN duh doo•wahn	
Quelle est la valeur ?	What's the value?
keh lay lah vah•luhr	
Qu'est-ce qu'il y a à l'intérieur ?	What's inside?
kehs keel•yah ah lehN•tay•reeyuhr	

Most locations of **la Poste** (the post office) are open from 8:00 a.m. to 7:00 or 8:00 p.m., Monday through Friday. On Saturdays, most post offices close at noon. In addition to standard postal services, you will also be able to bank at **la Poste**; ATMs can be found at many locations.

Food & Drink

Eating Out	59
Meals & Cooking	67
Drinks	84
On the Menu	89

ESSENTIAL

Can you recommend a good restaurant/bar?	**Pouvez-vous me conseiller un bon restaurant/bar ?** *poo•vay-voo muh kohN•say•yay uhN bohN reh•stoh•rawN/bahr*
Is there a traditional French/an inexpensive restaurant nearby?	**Y-a-t-il un restaurant traditionnel français/ bon marché près d'ici ?** *yah•teel uhN reh•stoh•rawN trah•dee•seeyohN•nehl frawN•say /bohN mahr•shay pray dee•see*
A table for…, please.	**Une table pour…, s'il vous plaît.** *ewn tah•bluh poor… seel voo play*
Can we sit…?	**Pouvons-nous nous asseoir…?** *poo•vohN•noo noo zah•swahr…*
here/there	**ici/là** *ee•see/lah*
outside	**dehors** *duh•ohr*
in a non-smoking area	**en zone non-fumeur** *awN zohn nohN•few•muhr*
I'm waiting for someone.	**J'attends quelqu'un.** *zhah•tawN kehl•kuhN*
Where are the toilets?	**Où sont les toilettes ?** *oo sohN lay twah•leht*
A menu, please.	**La carte, s'il vous plaît.** *lah kahrt seel voo play*
What do you recommend?	**Que recommandez-vous ?** *kuh reh•koh•mawN•day-voo*
I'd like…	**Je voudrais…** *zhuh voo•dray…*
Some more…, please.	**Un peu plus de…, s'il vous plaît.** *uhN puh plew duh… seel voo play*
Enjoy your meal!	**Bon appétit !** *bohN nah•peh•tee*

The check [bill], please.	**L'addition, s'il vous plaît.**
	lah•dee•seeyohN seel voo play
Is service included?	**Est-ce que le service est compris ?**
	ehs kuh luh sehr•vees ay kohN•pree
Can I pay by credit card/have a receipt?	**Puis-je payer par carte de crédit/avoir un reçu?** *pwee•zhuh pay•yay pahr kahrt duh kray•dee/ah•vwahr uhN ruh•sew*

Where to Eat

Can you recommend…?	**Pouvez-vous me conseiller…?**
	poo•vay•voo muh kohN•say•yay…
a restaurant	**un restaurant** *uhN reh•stoh•rawN*
a bar	**un bar** *uhN bahr*
a café	**un café** *uhN kah•fay*
a fast-food place	**un fast-food** *uhN fahst•food*
a cheap restaurant	**un restaurant bon marché**
	uhN reh•stoh•rawN bohN mahr•shay
an expensive restaurant	**un restaurant cher**
	uhN reh•stoh•rawN shehr
a restaurant with a good view	**un restaurant avec belle vue**
	uhN reh•stoh•rawN ah•vehk behl vew
an authentic/ a non-touristy restaurant	**un restaurant authentique / qui n'est pas envahi par les touristes**
	uhN reh•stoh•rawN oh•tawN•teek / kee nay pah awN•vah•yee pahr lay too•reest

Reservations & Preferences

| I'd like to reserve a table… | **Je voudrais réserver une table…** |
| | *zhuh voo•dray ray•zehr•vay ewn tah•bluh…* |

for two	**pour deux** *poor duh*
for this evening	**pour ce soir** *poor suh swahr*
for tomorrow at…	**pour demain à…** *poor duh•mehN ah…*
A table for two, please.	**Une table pour deux, s'il vous plaît.**
	ewn tah•bluh poor duh seel voo play
I have a reservation.	**J'ai une réservation.**
	zhay ewn ray•zehr•vah•seeyohN
My name is…	**Mon nom est…** *mohN nohN ay…*
Can we sit…?	**Pouvons-nous nous asseoir…?**
	poo•vohN•noo noo zah•swahr…
here/there	**ici/là** *ee•see/lah*
outside	**dehors** *duh•ohr*
in a non-smoking area	**en zone non-fumeur** *awN zohn nohN•few•muhr*
by the window	**à côté de la fenêtre** *ah koh•tay duh lah fuh•neh•truh*
in the shade	**à l'ombre** *ah lohN•bruh*
in the sun	**au soleil** *oh soh•lehy*
Where are the toilets?	**Où sont les toilettes ?** *oo sohN lay twah•leht*

YOU MAY HEAR...

Avez-vous réservé ?   Do you have a reservation?
ah·vay·voo ray·zehr·vay

Pour combien ?   How many?
poor kohN·beeyehN

Fumeur ou non-fumeur ?   Smoking or non-smoking?
few·muhr oo nohN·few·muhr

Êtes-vous prêts (à commander) ?   Are you ready (to order)?
eht·voo preh (ah koh·mawN·day)

Que désirez-vous ? *kuh day·zee·ray·voo*   What would you like?

Je vous conseille... *zhuh voo kohN·sehy...*   I recommend...

Bon appétit. *bohN nah·peh·tee*   Enjoy your meal.

How to Order

Excuse me, sir/ma'am?	**S'il vous plaît, monsieur/madame ?**
	seel voo play muh·seeyuhr/mah·dahm
We're ready (to order).	**Nous sommes prêts (à commander).**
	noo sohm preh (ah koh·mawN·day)
May I see the wine list?	**La liste des vins, s'il vous plaît.**
	lah leest day vehN seel voo play
I'd like...	**Je voudrais...** *zhuh voo·dray...*
a bottle of...	**une bouteille de...** *ewn boo·tehy duh...*
a carafe of...	**une carafe de...** *ewn kah·rahf duh...*
a glass of...	**un verre de...** *uhN vehr duh...*
Can I have a menu?	**La carte, s'il vous plaît.** *lah kahrt seel voo play*
Do you have...?	**Avez-vous...?** *ah·vay voo...*
a fixed-price menu	**un menu à prix fixe**
	uhN muh·new ah pree feeks

a menu in English	**un menu en anglais**	*uhN muh·new awN nawN·glay*
a children's menu	**un menu enfant**	*uhN muh·new awN·fawN*
What do you recommend?	**Que me conseillez-vous ?**	*kuh muh kohN·say·yay·voo*
What's this?	**Qu'est-ce que c'est ?**	*kehs kuh say*
What's in it?	**Quels sont les ingrédients ?**	*kehl sohN lay zehN·gray·deeyehN*
Is it spicy?	**C'est épicé ?**	*say ay·pee·say*
I'd like...	**Je voudrais...**	*zhuh voo·dray...*
More..., please.	**Plus..., s'il vous plaît.**	*plews...seel voo play*
With/Without...	**Avec/Sans...**	*ah·vehk/sawN...*
I can't eat...	**Je ne peux pas manger...**	*zhuh nuh puh pah mawN·zhay...*
rare	**saignant**	*say·nyawN*
medium	**à point**	*ah pwehN*
well-done	**bien cuit**	*beeyehN kwee*
It's to go [take away].	**C'est pour emporter.**	*say poor awN·pohr·tay*

For Drinks, see page 84.

YOU MAY SEE...

COUVERT	cover charge
PRIX FIXE	fixed-price
MENU (DU JOUR)	menu (of the day)
SERVICE (NON) COMPRIS	service (not) included
MENU À LA CARTE	specials

Cooking Methods

baked	**cuit** *kwee*
boiled	**bouilli** *boo·yee*
braised	**braisé** *bray·zay*
breaded	**en croute** *awN kroot*
creamed	**à la crème** *ah lah krehm*
diced	**en rondelles** *awN rohN·dehl*
filleted	**en filets** *awN fee·lay*
fried	**frit** *free*
grilled	**grillé** *gree·yay*
poached	**poché** *poh·shay*
roasted	**rôti** *roh·tee*
sautéed	**poêlé** *pwah·lay*
smoked	**fumé** *few·may*
steamed	**à la vapeur** *ah lah vah·puhr*
stewed	**mijoté** *mee·zhoh·tay*
stuffed	**farci** *fahr·see*

Dietary Requirements

I'm...	**Je suis...** *zhuh swee...*
diabetic	**diabétique** *deeyah·beh·teek*
lactose intolerant	**allergique au lactose** *ah·lehr·zheek oh lahk·tohz*
vegetarian	**végétarien m /végétarienne f** *vay·zhay·tah·reeyehN /vay·zhay·tah·reeyehn*
vegan	**végétalien m / végétalienne f** *vay·zhay·tah·leeyehN / vay·zhay·tah·leeyehn*
I'm allergic to...	**Je suis allergique à...** *zhuh swee ah·lehr·zheek ah...*
I can't eat...	**Je ne peux pas manger...** *zhuh nuh puh pah mawN·zhay...*

dairy products	**de produits laitiers** *duh proh·dwee lay·teeyay*
gluten	**de gluten** *duh glew·tawN*
nuts	**des noix** *day nwah*
pork	**du porc** *dew pohr*
shellfish	**des fruits de mer** *day frwee duh mehr*
spicy foods	**de la nourriture épicée**
	duh lah noo·ree·tewr ay·pee·say
wheat	**du blé** *dew blay*
Is it halal/kosher?	**Est-ce que c'est halal/casher ?**
	ehs kuh say ah·lahl/kah·shehr
Do you have…?	**Avez-vous…?** *ah·vay voo…*
skimmed milk	**du lait écrémé** *dew lay ay·kray·may*
whole milk	**du lait entier** *dew lay awN·teeyay*
soya milk	**du lait de soja** *dew lay duh soh·zhah*

Dining with Children

Do you have children's portions?	**Faites-vous des portions enfants ?** *feht·voo day pohr·seeyohN awN·fawN*
Can I have a highchair/child's seat?	**Une chaise haute pour bébé/Un siège pour enfant, s'il vous plaît.**
	ewn shay zoht poor bay·bay/uhN seeyehzh poo rawN·fawN seel voo play
Where can I feed/ change the baby?	**Où puis-je allaiter/changer le bébé ?** *oo pwee·zhuh ah·leh·tay/shawN·zhay luh bay·bay*
Can you warm this?	**Pouvez-vous réchauffer ceci ?** *poo·vay·voo ray·shoh·fay suh·see*

For Traveling with Children, see page 148.

How to Complain

When will our food be ready?	**Dans combien de temps serons-nous servis ?** *dawN kohN•beeyehN duh tawN suh•rohN•noo sehr•vee*
We can't wait any longer.	**Nous ne pouvons plus attendre.** *noo nuh poo•vohN plew zhah•tawN•druh*
We're leaving.	**Nous partons.** *noo pahr•tohN*
I didn't order this.	**Ce n'est pas ce que j'ai commandé.** *suh nay pah suh kuh zhay koh•mawN•day*
I ordered...	**J'ai commandé...** *zhay koh•mawN•day...*
I can't eat this.	**Je ne peux pas manger ça.** *zhuh nuh puh pah mawN•zhay sah*
This is too...	**C'est trop...** *say troh...*
cold/hot	**froid/chaud** *frwah/shoh*
salty/spicy	**salé/épicé** *sah•lay/ay•pee•say*
tough/bland	**dur/sans goût** *dewr/sawN goo*
This isn't clean/fresh.	**Ce n'est pas propre/frais.** *suh nay pah proh•pruh/fray*

Paying

The check [bill], please.	**L'addition, s'il vous plaît.** *lah•dee•seeyohN seel voo play*
Separate checks day [bills], please.	**Des additions séparées, s'il vous plaît.** *zah•dee•seeyohN say•pah•ray seel voo play*
It's all together.	**C'est ensemble.** *say tawN•sawN•bluh*
Is service included?	**Le service est-il compris ?** *luh sehr•vees ay•teel kohN•pree*
What's this amount for?	**À quoi correspond ce montant ?** *ah kwah koh•rhes•pohN suh mohN•tawN*

I didn't have that.	**Je n'ai pas eu ceci. J'ai eu...**
I had...	*zhuh nay pah ew suh•see zhay ew...*
Can I have a receipt/	**Puis-je avoir un reçu/reçu détaillé ?**
an itemized bill?	*pwee•zhuh ah•vwahr uhN ruh•sew/ruh•sew*
	day•tie•yay
That was delicious!	**C'était délicieux !** *seh•tay day•lee•seeyuh*
I've already paid.	**J'ai déjà payé.** *zhay day•zhah pay•yay*

Service is included in the price at cafes and restaurants. However, people do tend to leave a small tip. Round up the bill to the nearest euro or two for good service.

Meals & Cooking

Le petit déjeuner (breakfast) is usually served from 7:00 a.m. until 10:00 a.m. and is a light meal, such as bread with butter and jam and coffee or tea. **Le déjeuner** (lunch) is usually served from noon until 2:00 p.m. and can be a full sit-down meal or a fast meal on the go, whichever you have time for. A picnic lunch is popular, and all the fixings can be found at the local bakery, butcher and wine store. **Le goûter** (snack), perhaps a croissant or pieces of chocolate, is common in the afternoon, especially for children. **Le dîner** (dinner) is usually served between 7:00 p.m. and 10:00 p.m. This often is a multi-course meal, served with wine, and enjoyed at a leisurely pace.

Breakfast

le bacon *luh beh·kohn*	bacon
le beurre *luh buhr*	butter
le café/thé… *luh kah·fay/tay…*	coffee/tea…
noir *nwahr*	black
déca *day·kah*	decaf
au lait *oh lay*	with milk
avec du sucre *ah·vehk dew sew·kruh*	with sugar
avec de l'édulcorant	with artificial
ah·vehk duh lay·dewl·koh·rawN	sweetener
les céréales chaudes/froides	cold/hot cereal
lay say·ray·ahl shohd/frwahd	
la charcuterie *lah shahr·kew·tuh·ree*	cold cuts
le croissant *luh krwah·sawN*	croissant
la confiture *lah kohN·fee·tewr*	jam/jelly
le fromage *luh froh·mahzh*	cheese
le jus… *luh zhew…*	…juice
d'orange *doh·rawNzh*	orange
de pommes *duh pohm*	apple
de pamplemousse	grapefruit
duh pawN·pluh·moos	

le lait *luh lay*	milk
l'avoine *lah·vwahn*	oatmeal
l'eau *loh*	water
le muesli *luh mews·lee*	granola [muesli]
le muffin *luh muh·feen*	muffin
l'œuf... *luhf...*	...egg
dur/à la coque *dewr/ah lah kohk*	hard-/soft-boiled
sur le plat *sewr luh plah*	fried
brouillé *broo·yay*	scrambled
l'omelette *lohm·leht*	omelet
le pain *luh pehN*	bread
le pain grillé *luh pehN gree·yay*	toast
le petit pain *luh puh·tee pehN*	roll
la saucisse *lah soh·sees*	sausage
le yaourt *luh yah·oort*	yogurt

Appetizers

les acras *lay zhah·krah*	small, fried fritters made from cod
l'andouille *lawN·doohy*	seasoned sausage, served grilled or fried
la bouchée à la reine *lah boo·shay ah lah rehn*	pastry shell filled with creamed sweetbreads and mushrooms
les crudités variées *lay krew·dee·tay vah·reeyay*	assorted vegetables in a vinaigrette dressing
les escargots *lay zehs·kahr·goh*	snails
le foie gras *luh fwah grah*	fresh goose liver
le pâté *luh pah·tay*	liver paté

les quenelles *lay kuh·nehl*	light dumplings made of fish, fowl or meat, in cream sauce
les quenelles de brochet *lay kuh·nehl duh broh·shay*	dumplings made of pike in cream sauce
la quiche *lah keesh*	an open-faced egg and cheese tart filled with vegetables, meat or seafood
la quiche lorraine *lah keesh loh·rayn*	open-faced egg and cheese tart filled with bacon
les rillettes *lay ree·yeht*	pork mixture served as a spread for bread
la terrine *lah teh·reen*	pâté made from pork, poultry, game or fish
les toasts *lay tohst*	toasted pieces of bread with different toppings

Soup

l'aïgo boulido *lah·ee·goh boolee·doh*	garlic soup, a specialty of Provence
la bisque *lah beesk*	seafood stew
la bouillabaisse *lah boo·yah·behs*	seafood soup, a specialty of Marseilles
le consommé *luh kohN·soh·may*	clear soup
le consommé Célestine *luh kohN·soh·may say·lehs·teen*	clear soup with chicken and noodles
le consommé Colbert *luh kohN·soh·may kohl·behr*	clear soup with poached eggs, spring vegetables
le consommé à l'œuf *luh kohN·soh·may ah luhf*	clear soup with a raw egg

le consommé au porto   clear soup with port wine
luh kohN•soh•may oh pohr•toh

la garbure *lah gahr•bewr*   cabbage soup, often with pork or goose

le potage à l'ail *luh poh•tahzh ah lie*   garlic soup

le potage du barry   cream of cauliflower soup
luh poh•tahzh dew bah•ree

le potage bilibi *luh poh•tahzh bee•lee•bee*   fish and oyster soup

le potage bonne ferme   soup with potatoes, bohn
luh poh•tahzh fehrm   leeks and sometimes bacon

le potage condé *luh poh•tahzh kohN•day*   soup with mashed red beans

le potage crécy *luh poh•tahzh kray•see*   soup with carrots and rice

le potage au cresson *luh poh•tahzh*   watercress soup
oh kreh•sohN

le potage julienne   shredded vegetable soup
luh poh•tahzh zhew•leeyehn

le potage Parmentier   potato soup
luh poh•tahzh pahr•mawN•teeyay

le pot-au-feu *luh poh-toh-fuh*   meat and vegetable stew

le ragoût *luh rah•goo*   thick stew

la soupe à la bière   beer soup with chicken
lah soop ah lah beeyehr   stock and onions

la soupe aux choux *lah soop oh shoo*   cabbage soup

la soupe de haricots   bean soup
lah soop duh ah•ree•koh

la soupe aux légumes   vegetable soup
lah soop oh lay•gewm

la soupe à l'oignon *lah soop ah loh•nyohN*   French onion soup

la soupe au pistou *lah soop oh pees•too*   basil-vegetable soup, a specialty of Provence

la soupe de poulet *lah soop duh poo•lay*   chicken soup

la soupe de poisson   soup with small fish,
lah soop duh pwah•sohN   simmered and pureed
la soupe de tomates *lah soop duh toh•maht*   tomato soup
la soupe de volaille *lah soop duh voh•lie*   chicken soup
le velouté *luh vuh•loo•tay*   cream soup

Fish & Seafood

le anchois *luh awN•shwah*   anchovy
l'anguille *lawN•geeyuh*   eel
le bar *luh bahr*   bass
le bar aux herbes en chemise   bass stuffed with
luh bah roh zayrb awN sheh•meez   spinach and herbs,
    wrapped in lettuce and
    poached in white wine
le brochet *luh broh•shay*   pike
le calmar *luh kahl•mahr*   squid
les coquilles Saint-Jacques   breaded scallops sautéed
lay koh•keeyuh sehN•zhahk   in lemon juice and herbs
le crabe *luh krahb*   crab
la crevette *lah kruh•veht*   shrimp
la dorade *lah doh•rahd*   sea bass
l'écrevisse *lay•kruh•vees*   crawfish
l'escargot *lehs•kahr•goh*   snail
l'espadon *leh•spah•dohN*   swordfish
le flétan *luh flay•tawN*   halibut
le hareng *luh ah•rawN*   herring
le homard *luh oh•mahr*   lobster
le homard cardinal   lobster cooked with
luh oh•mahr kahr•dee•nahl   mushrooms and truffles
    in a béchamel sauce

l'huître *luh wee•truh*	oyster
la morue *lah moh•rew*	cod
la moule *lah mool*	mussel
les moules marinières *lay mool mah•ree•neeyehr*	mussels in white wine sauce
la palourde *lah pah•loord*	clam
le plateau de fruits de mer *luh plah•toh duh frwee duh mehr*	assorted seafood platter
le poulpe *luh poolp*	octopus
la sardine *lah sahr•deen*	sardine
le saumon *luh soh•mohN*	salmon
le saumon à l'oseille *luh soh•mohN ah loh•zehy*	salmon with sorrel sauce
la sole *lah sohl*	sole
le thon *luh tohN*	tuna
la truite *lah trweet*	trout
la truite aux amandes *lah trweet oh zah•mawNd*	trout sautéed in a creamy almond sauce
la truite meunière *lah trweet muh•neeyehr*	seasoned, breaded trout, pan-fried in butter

Meat & Poultry

l'agneau *lah·nyoh*	lamb
le bacon *luh beh·kohn*	bacon
le bifteck *luh beef·tehk*	steak
le bœuf *luh buhf*	beef
la caille *lah kie*	quail
le canard *luh kah·nahr*	duck
le canard à l'orange *luh kah·nahr ah loh·rawNzh*	duck braised with orange liqueur
le cassoulet toulousain *luh kah·soo·lay too·loo·zehN*	casserole of white beans, mutton or salt pork, sausage and preserved goose
le cervela *luh sehr·vuh·lah*	garlic pork sausage
le chevreuil *luh shuh·vruhy*	venison
le cochon de lait *luh koh·shohN duh lay*	suckling pig
le coq au vin *luh koh koh vehN*	chicken in red wine sauce
la côtelette de porc *lah koh·tuh·leht duh pohr*	pork chop
la dinde *lah dehNd*	turkey
l'épaule d'agneau farcie *lay·pohl dah·nyoh fahr·see*	stuffed lamb shoulder
l'escalope de veau normande *lehs·kah·lohp duh voh nohr·mawNd*	thinly sliced veal in cream sauce
l'escalope de veau milanaise *lehs·kah·lohp duh voh mee·lah·nehz*	thinly sliced veal in tomato sauce
le faisan *luh fay·zawN*	pheasant
le foie *luh fwah*	liver
le jambon *luh zhawN·bohN*	ham

le lapin *luh lah-pehN*	rabbit
le lapin à la Lorraine	rabbit in a mushroom
luh lah-pehN ah lah loh-rehn	cream sauce
le lapin à la moutarde	rabbit in mustard sauce
luh lah-pehN ah lah moo-tahrd	
les lardons *lay lahr-dohN*	cubes of salt pork
le porc *luh pohr*	pork
le poulet *luh poo-lay*	chicken
le poulet à l'estragon	chicken in a tarragon
luh poo-lay ah lehs-trah-gohN	cream sauce
le poulet chasseur *luh poo-lay shah-suhr*	chicken in a mushroom
	wine sauce
le ris *luh rees*	sweetbreads
la saucisse *lah soh-sees*	sausage
le steak *luh stayk*	steak
le tournedos *luh toor-nuh-doh*	small filet of beef
le veau *luh voh*	veal

Vegetables & Staples

l'ail *lie*	garlic
l'artichaut *lahr-tee-shoh*	artichoke
les asperges *lay zah-spehrzh*	asparagus
l'aubergine *loh-behr-zheen*	eggplant [aubergine]
l'avocat *lah-voh-kah*	avocado
le brocoli *luh broh-koh-lee*	broccoli
la carotte *lah kah-roht*	carrot
les carottes vichy	carrots sauteed in butter
lay kah-roht vee-shee	
le céleri *luh say-luh-ree*	celery
le champignon *luh shawN-pee-nyohN*	mushroom

le chou *luh shoo*	cabbage
les choux verts à l'anglaise	julienned cabbage,
lay shoo vehr ah lawN·glehz	sautéed in butter
le chou-fleur *luh shoo·fluhr*	cauliflower
le chou-fleur au gratin	baked cauliflower,
luh shoo·fluhr oh grah·tehN	covered in cheese
la courgette *lah koor·zheht*	zucchini [courgette]
les épinards *lay zay·pee·nahr*	spinach
les épinards à la crème	creamed spinach
lay zay·pee·nahr ah lah krehm	
les haricots *lay ah·ree·koh*	beans
les haricots verts *lay ah·ree·koh vehr*	green beans
la laitue *lah lay·tew*	lettuce
les légumes *lay lay·gewm*	vegetables
le maïs *luh mah·ees*	corn
l'oignon *loh·nyohN*	onion
l'olive *loh·leev*	olive
les pâtes *lay paht*	pasta
les petits pois *lay puh·tee pwah*	peas
le poivron rouge/vert	red/green pepper
roozh/ luh pwah·vrohN vehr	

les poivrons farcis	stuffed green peppers
lay pwah•vrohN fahr•see	
la pomme de terre *lah pohm duh tehr*	potato
salade... *sah•lahd...*	salad...
antiboise *ahN•tee•bwahz*	with anchovy, green pepper, beets, rice and capers
niçoise *nee•swahz*	with tuna, anchovy, olives and vegetables
russe *rews*	with diced vegetables
de thon *duh tohN*	with tuna
verte *vehrt*	with mixed greens
le riz *luh ree*	rice
la tomate *lah toh•maht*	tomato

Fruit

l'abricot *lah•bree•koh*	apricot
l'ananas *lah•nah•nah*	pineapple
la banane *lah bah•nahn*	banana
le cassis *luh kah•sees*	black currant
la cerise *lah suh•reez*	cherry
le citron *luh see•trohN*	lemon
le citron vert *luh see•trohN vehr*	lime
la fraise *lah frehz*	strawberry
la framboise *lah frawN•bwahz*	raspberry
le fruit *luh frwee*	fruit
la groseille *lah groh•zehy*	red currant
le melon *luh muh•lohN*	melon
la myrtille *lah meer•teeyuh*	blueberry
l'orange *loh•rawNzh*	orange

le pamplemousse *luh pawN·pluh·moos*	grapefruit
la pêche *lah pehsh*	peach
la poire *lah pwahr*	pear
la pomme *lah pohm*	apple
la prune *lah prewn*	plum
le raisin *luh reh·zehN*	grape

Cheese

le banon *luh bah·nohN*	mild goat's and cow's milk cheese with a nutty flavor
le bleu d'auvergne *luh bluh doh·vehr·nyuh*	cow's milk blue cheese with a strong flavor
le brie *luh bree*	soft cheese, ranging in strength and flavors
le camembert *luh kah·mawN·behr*	soft, raw cow's milk cheese
le coulommiers *luh koo·luh·meeyay*	soft, mild cow's milk cheese
la fondue *lah fohN·dew*	a pot of melted cheese dip
le fromage *luh froh·mahzh*	cheese
le fromage blanc *luh froh·mahzh blawN*	rich, creamy white cheese eaten for breakfast topped with cream and sugar
le fromage de chèvre *luh froh·mahzh duh sheh·vruh*	goat's milk cheese
le munster *luh muhN·stuhr*	soft, spicy cow's milk cheese from Alsace
le roquefort *luh rohk·fohr*	blue, soft and pungent sheep's milk cheese
le Saint-Paulin *luh sehN·poh·lehN*	smooth and mild cow's milk cheese

Dessert

la crêpe... *lah krehp...* — thin pancake...
    à la confiture *ah lah kohN•fee•tewr* — with jam
    au sucre *oh sew•kruh* — with sugar
    suzette *sew•zeht* — in an orange-flavored sauce

le beignet *luh beh•nyay* — deep fried dough
le diplomate *luh dee•ploh•maht* — molded custard with fruit, lined with sponge cake that has been steeped in liqueur

le gâteau au fromage *luh gah•toh oh froh•mahzh* — cheesecake
la génoise *lah zhay•nwahz* — sponge cake
le mont-blanc *luh mohN•blawN* — pastry with chestnut purée, whipped cream and meringue

la mousse au chocolat *lah moos oh shoh•koh•lah* — chocolate mousse
les petits fours *lay pu•tee foor* — bite-sized, decorated pastries

la poire belle-hélène *lah pwahr behl•ehl•ehn* — poached pears with ice cream and chocolate sauce

le sabayon *luh sah•bah•yohN* — creamy dessert made from egg yolks, wine, sugar and flavoring

la tarte aux fruits *lah tahrt oh frwee* — fruit pie or tart
la tarte tatin *lah tahrt tah•tehN* — upside down baked apple tart

Sauces & Condiments

à la bonne femme *ah lah bohn fehm*	white wine sauce with vegetables
béarnaise *beh·ahr·nehz*	a sauce made with butter, eggs, shallots, wine and tarragon
bordelaise *bohr·duh·lehz*	sauce made with Bordeaux wine
chantilly *shawN·tee·yee*	sauce made with whipping cream
estragon *eh·strah·gohN*	with tarragon
florentine *floh·rawN·teen*	with spinach
hollandaise *oh·lawN·dehz*	creamy egg yolk and butter sauce
normande *nohr·mawNd*	fish sauce with shrimp or oysters
rémoulade *ray·moo·lahd*	mayonnaise mixed with mustard
sel *sehl*	salt
poivre *pwah·vruh*	pepper
moutarde *moo·tahrd*	mustard
ketchup *Ket·shuhp*	ketchup

At the Market

Where are the trolleys/baskets?	**Où sont les chariots/paniers ?** *oo sohN lay shah·reeyoh/pah·neeyay*
Where is…?	**Où est…?** *oo ay…*
I'd like some of that/this.	**Je voudrais un peu de cela/ceci.** *zhuh voo·dray zuhN puh duh suh·lah/suh·see*
Can I taste it?	**Puis-je goûter ?** *pwee·zhuh goo·tay*

I'd like...	**Je voudrais...** *zhuh voo·dray...*
a kilo/half-kilo of...	**un kilo/demi-kilo de...**
	uhN kee·loh/ duh·mee·kee·loh duh...
a liter of...	**un litre de...** *uhN lee·truh duh...*
a piece of...	**une pièce de...** *ewn peeyehs duh...*
a slice of...	**un morceau de...** *uhN mohr·soh duh...*
More./Less.	**Plus./Moins.** *plews/mwehN*
How much?	**Combien ça coûte ?** *kohN·beeyehN sah koot*
Where do I pay?	**Où dois-je payer ?** *oo dwah·zhuh pay·yay*
A bag, please.	**Un sachet, s'il vous plaît.**
	uhN sah·shay seel voo play
I'm being helped.	**On me sert.** *ohN muh sehr*

For Conversion Tables, see page 178.

YOU MAY HEAR...

Puis-je vous aider? *pwee·zhuh voo zay·day*	Can I help you?
Que voulez-vous? *kuh voo·lay·voo*	What would you like?
Autre chose? *oh·truh shohz*	Anything else?
Ça fait...euros. *Sah fay...uh·roh*	That's...euros.

Local markets—indoor and outdoor—are a wonderful way to discover fresh, seasonal and regional products and to get a hint of the French way of life. Both sell a variety of products such as cheese, meat, flowers, homemade preserves, honey, nuts and farm fresh vegetables, fruit, eggs and more.

Measurements in Europe are metric - and that applies to the weight of food too. If you tend to think in pounds and ounces, it's worth brushing up on what the metric equivalent is before you go shopping for fruit and veg in markets and supermarkets. Five hundred grams, or half a kilo, is a common quantity to order, and that converts to just over a pound (17.65 ounces, to be precise).

YOU MAY SEE...

À CONSOMMER DE PRÉFÉRENCE AVANT LE...	best if used by...
KILOCALORIES	calories
0% DE MATIÈRES GRASSES	fat free
CONSERVER AU RÉFRIGÉRATEUR	keep refrigerated
PEUT CONTENIR DES TRACES DE...	may contain traces of...
VA AU MICRO-ONDE	microwaveable
DATE LIMITE DE VENTE...	sell by...
CONVIENT AUX VÉGÉTARIENS	suitable for vegetarians

In the Kitchen

bottle opener	**un décapsuleur** *uhN day·kahp·sew·luhr*
bowl	**un saladier** *uhN sah·lah·deeyay*
can opener	**un ouvre-boîte** *uhN oo·vruh·bwaht*
corkscrew	**un tire-bouchon** *uhN teer·boo·shohN*
cup	**une tasse** *ewn tahs*
fork	**une fourchette** *ewn foor·sheht*
frying pan	**une poêle** *ewn pwahl*
glass	**un verre** *uhN vehr*
(steak) knife	**un couteau (à steak)** *uhN koo·toh (ah stayk)*
measuring cup/ spoon	**une mesure/cuillère à doser** *ewn meh·zewr/kwee·yehr ah doh·say*
napkin	**une serviette** *ewn sayr·veeyeht*
plate	**une assiette** *ewn ah·seeyeht*
pot	**une casserole** *ewn kah·suh·rohl*
spatula	**une spatule** *ewn spah·tewl*
spoon	**une cuillère** *ewn kwee·yehr*

Drinks

ESSENTIAL

Can I see the wine list /drinks menu, please?	**La carte des vins/boissons, s'il vous plaît.** *lah kahrt day vehN/bwah•sohN seel voo play*
What do you recommend?	**Que me conseillez-vous ?** *kuh muh kohN•say•yay•voo*
I'd like a bottle/glass of red/white wine.	**Je voudrais une bouteille/un verre de vin rouge/blanc.** *zhuh voo•dray ewn boo•tehy/uhN vehr duh vehN roozh/blawN*
The house wine, please.	**Le vin de la maison, s'il vous plaît.** *luh vehN duh lah may•zohN seel voo play*
Another bottle/glass, please.	**Une autre bouteille/Un autre verre, s'il vous plaît.** *ewn oh•truh boo•tehy/uhN noh•truh vehr seel voo play*
I'd like a local beer.	**Je voudrais une bière locale.** *zhuh voo•dray ewn beeyehr loh•kahl*
Can I buy you a drink?	**Puis-je vous offrir un verre ?** *pwee•zhuh voo zoh•freer uhN vehr*
Cheers!	**Santé!** *sawN•tay*
A coffee/tea, please.	**Un café/thé, s'il vous plaît.** *uhN kah•fay/tay seel voo play*
Black.	**Noir.** *nwahr*
With...	**Avec...** *ah•vehk...*
milk	**du lait** *dew lay*
sugar	**du sucre** *dew sew•kruh*
artificial sweetener	**de l'édulcorant** *duh lay•dewl•koh•rawN*
A..., please.	**Un..., s'il vous plaît.** *uhN... seel voo play*
juice	**jus de fruit** *zhew duh frwee*
soda	**soda** *soh•dah*

Sparkling/still water	**de l'eau gazeuse/plate** *duh loh gah·zuhz/plaht*

Non-alcoholic Drinks

le café *luh kah·fay*	coffee
le chocolat chaud *luh shoh·koh·lah shoh*	hot chocolate
la citronnade *lah see·troh·nahd*	lemonade
l'eau gazeuse/plate *loh gah·zuhz/plaht*	sparkling/still water
le jus de fruit *luh zhew duh frwee*	juice
le lait *luh lay*	milk
le soda *luh soh·dah*	soda
le thé (glacé) *luh tay (glah·say)*	(iced) tea

France offers a wide choice of mineral water. Popular French brands include Evian®, Vittel®, Volvic® and Badoit®; Perrier® and Vichy® are popular sparkling waters.

Café (espresso-style coffee) is also very popular. **Café** in France is not typically 'to go.' The French will enjoy their **café** while sitting with friends or just 'people-watching.' **Thé** (tea) is available and can be served **au lait** (with milk), **au citron** (with lemon), **à la menthe** (with mint leaves) or **glacé** (iced). **Tisane** (herbal tea) is also popular.

YOU MAY HEAR...

Voulez-vous boire quelque chose ?
voo·lay·voo bwahr kehl·kuh shohz

Can I get you a drink?

Avec du lait ou du sucre ?
ah·vehk dew lay oo dew sew·kruh

With milk or sugar?

De l'eau gazeuse ou plate ?
duh loh gah·zuhz oo plaht

Sparkling or still water?

Aperitifs, Cocktails & Liqueurs

le cognac *luh koh·nyahk*	brandy
le gin *luh zheen*	gin
le rhum *luh ruhm*	rum
le scotch *luh skoh·tsh*	scotch
la tequila *lah teh·kee·lah*	tequila
la vodka *lah vohd·kah*	vodka
le whisky *luh wees·kee*	whisky

Apéritifs are much more common than cocktails. Many are wine- and brandy-based with herbs and bitters; popular brands are Amer Picon®, Byrrh®, Dubonnet®, Pernod® and Ricard®.
Fruit-distilled brandies are popular as after-dinner drinks: calvados (apple), **kirsch** (cherry), **marc** (grape), **poire William** (pear) or **quetsche** (plum). Other popular liqueurs include the famous orange-flavored Grand Marnier® and Cointreau®.

Beer

la bière... *lah beeyehr...*	...beer
en bouteille/pression	bottled/draft
awN boo·tehy/preh·seeyohN	
brune/blonde *brewn/blohNd*	dark/light
blonde/pils *blohNd/peels*	lager/pilsener
locale/importée *loh·kahl/ehN·pohr·tay*	local/imported
non-alcoolisée *noh·nahl·koo·lee·zay*	non-alcoholic

Wine

le vin... *luh vehN...*	...wine
rouge/blanc *roozh/blawN*	red/white
de maison/de table	house/table
duh may·zohN/duh tah·bluh	
sec/sucré *sehk/sew·kray*	dry/sweet
pétillant *pay·tee·yawN*	sparkling
le champagne *luh shawN·pah·nyuh*	champagne
le vin de dessert *luh vehN duh day·sehr*	dessert wine

French wine is world-renowned. In restaurants, a **sommelier** (wine waiter) can offer advice on wine selections that will pair well with your meal—a tip is appreciated for this service.

Region	Main grape varieties	Popular wine styles
Alsace	Riesling, Pinot Blanc, Gewürztraminer	dry, semi-dry and sweet white wines
Bordeaux	Merlot, Cabernet-Sauvignon, Sémillon, Sauternes	full- and medium-bodied dry red wine; white dessert wine
Burgundy	Pinot Noir, Gamay, Chardonnay	full- and medium-bodied dry red wine; full-bodied dry white wine
Champagne	Chardonnay, Pinot Meunier, Pinot Noir	sparkling wine ranging from sweet to very dry
Côtes du Rhône	Grenache, Syrah, Viognier, Clairette	diverse red wine, from fruity to robust; full-bodied dry white wine
Languedoc-Roussillon	Carignan, Grenache, Mourvèdre, Cinsault, Merlot, Syrah	fine and table red wine; semi-dry and dry rosé wine; sweet white wine
Loire	Chenin Blanc, Sauvignon, Muscadet	lighter, dry and semi-dry white wine; some rosé and fruity red wine
Provence	Cinsault, Grenache, Mourvèdre, Syrah	dry and fruity rosé wine; full-bodied dry red wine; some white wine
Corsica	Nieluccio, Sciacarello, Vermentino,	dry rosé and red wine; light, dry white wine
Southwest France	Cabernet, Merlot, Sémillon, Sauvignon	full-bodied dry red wine; flavorful white wine

On the Menu

les abats *lay zah·bah*	organ meat [offal]
les abattis *lay zah·bah·tee*	giblets
l'abricot *lah·bree·koh*	apricot
l'agneau *lah·nyoh*	lamb
l'ail *lie*	garlic
l'amande *lah·mawNd*	almond
l'ananas *lah·nah·nah*	pineapple
l'anchois *lawN·shwah*	anchovy
l'andouillette *lawN·doo·yett*	French sausage
l'aneth *lah·neht*	dill
l'anguille *lawN·gheeyuh*	eel
l'artichaut *lahr·tee·shoh*	artichoke
l'asperge *lah·spehrzh*	asparagus
l'aubergine *loh·buhr·zheen*	eggplant [aubergine]
l'avocat *lah·voh·kah*	avocado
le babeurre *luh bah·buhr*	buttermilk
le bacon *luh beh·kohN*	bacon
la banane *lah bah·nahn*	banana
le bar *luh bahr*	sea bass

le basilic *luh bah·see·leek*	basil
la baudroie *lah boh·drwah*	monkfish
le beignet *luh beh·nyay*	fritter
la betterave *lah beh·tuh·rahv*	beet
le beurre *luh buhr*	butter
la bière *lah beeyehr*	beer
le bifteck d'aloyau	sirloin
luh beef·tehk dah·lwah·yoh	
le biscuit *luh bees·kwee*	cookie [biscuit]
le blé *luh blay*	wheat
le bleu *luh bluh*	blue cheese
le bœuf *luh buhf*	beef
les bonbons *lay bohN·bohN*	candy [sweets]
le boudin *luh boo·dehN*	blood sausage
le bouillon *luh boo·yohN*	broth
le cabillaud *luh kah·beeyoh*	haddock
la cacahuète *lah kah·kah·weht*	peanut
le café *luh kah·fay*	coffee
la caille *lah kie*	quail
le calmar *luh kahl·mahr*	squid
le canard *luh kah·nahr*	duck

la canneberge *lah kah·nuh·behrzh*	cranberry
la cannelle *lah kah·nehl*	cinnamon
la câpre *lah kah·pruh*	caper
le caramel *luh kah·rah·mehl*	caramel
la carotte *lah kah·roht*	carrot
le cassis *luh kah·sees*	black currant
le céleri *luh say·luh·ree*	celery
les céréales *lay say·ray·ahl*	cereal
la cerise *lah suh·reez*	cherry
la chair de crabe *lah shehr duh krahb*	crabmeat
le champignon *luh shawN·pee·nyohN*	mushroom
la charcuterie *lah shar·kew·tuh·ree*	cold cuts
la chèvre *lah sheh·vruh*	goat
le chevreau *luh shuh·vroh*	kid (young goat)
la chicorée *lah shee·koh·ray*	chicory
les chips *lay sheeps*	potato chips [crisps]
le chocolat *luh shoh·koh·lah*	chocolate
le chou *luh shoo*	cabbage
le chou rouge *luh shoo roozh*	red cabbage
le chou-fleur *luh shoo·fluhr*	cauliflower
les choux de Bruxelles *lay shoo duh brewk·sehl*	Brussels sprouts
la ciboule *lah see·bool*	scallion [spring onion]
le cidre *luh see·druh*	cider
le citron *luh see·trohN*	lemon
le citron vert *luh see·trohN vehr*	lime
la citrouille *lah see·truhy*	pumpkin
les cives *lay seev*	chives
le clou de girofle *luh kloo duh zhee·roh·fluh*	clove
le cœur *luh kuhr*	heart
le cognac *luh koh·nyahk*	brandy

le colin *luh koh•lehN*	hake
la compote *lah kohN•poht*	stewed fruit
le concombre *luh kohN•kohN•bruh*	cucumber
la confiture *lah kohN•fee•tewr*	jam
les coquillages *lay koh•kee•yahzh*	shellfish
les coquilles *lay koh•keeyuh*	scallops
la coriandre *lah koh•reeyawN•druh*	cilantro [coriander]
le cornichon *luh kohr•nee•shohN*	gherkin/pickle
la côtelette *lah koh•teh•leht*	chop
la courgette *lah koor•zheht*	zucchini [courgette]
le crabe *luh krahb*	crab
la crème *lah krehm*	cream
la crème aigre *lah krehm eh•gruh*	sour cream
la crème anglaise *lah krehm awN•glehz*	custard
la crème fouettée *lah krehm fooweh•tay*	cream, whipped
la crème fraîche *lah krehm frehsh*	heavy cream
la crêpe *lah krehp*	pancake
le cresson *luh kruh•sohN*	watercress
la crevette *lah kruh•veht*	shrimp/prawn
le croissant *luh krwah•sawN*	croissant
le cumin *luh kew•mehN*	cumin
le cumin de près *luh kew•mehN*	caraway *duh preh*
la datte *lah daht*	date
la dinde *lah dehNd*	turkey
la dorade *lah doh•rahd*	sea bass
l'eau *loh*	water
l'eau tonique *loh toh•neek*	tonic water
l'échalote *lay•shah•loht*	shallot
l'edulcorant *lay•dewl•koh•rawN*	artificial sweetener
l'endive *lawN•deev*	endive
l'épaule *lay•pohl*	shoulder

les épices *lay zay•pees*	spices
les épinards *lay zay•pee•nahr*	spinach
l'escalope (de poulet)	breast (of chicken)
lehs•kah•lohp (duh poo•lay)	
l'escargot *lehs•kahr•goh*	snail
l'écrevisse *lay•kruh•vees*	crayfish
l'espadon *lehs•pah•dohN*	swordfish
l'estragon *lehs•trah•gohN*	tarragon
le faisan *luh feh•zawN*	pheasant
le fenouil *luh fuh•noohy*	fennel
la feuille de laurier	bay leaf
lah fuhy duh loh•reeyay	
la figue *lah feeg*	fig
le filet *luh fee•lay*	loin
les fines herbes *lay feen zayrb*	herbs
les flageolets *lay flah•zheh•lay*	bean sprouts
le flétan *luh flay•tawN*	halibut
le foie *luh fwah*	liver
la fraise *lah frehz*	strawberry
la framboise *lah frawN•bwahz*	raspberry
les frites *lay freet*	French fries

le fromage *luh froh•mahzh*	cheese
le fromage blanc *luh froh•mahzh blawN*	soft, creamy cheese
le fromage de chèvre	goat cheese
luh froh•mahzh duh sheh•vruh	
le fromage frais *luh froh•mahzh fray*	soft, new cheese
le fruit *luh frwee*	fruit
les fruits de mer *lay frwee duh mehr*	seafood
le gâteau *luh gah•toh*	cake
le gâteau sec *luh gah•toh sehk*	cracker
la gaufre *lah goh•fruh*	waffle
la geléelah *zhuh•lay*	jelly
le gibier *luh zhee•beeyay*	game
le gigot *luh zhee•goh*	leg
le gin *luh zheen*	gin
le gingembre *luh zhehN•zhawN•bruh*	ginger
la glace *lah glahs*	ice cream
le glaçon *luh glah•sohN*	ice (cube)
les gombos *lay gohN•boh*	okra
le goûter *luh goo•tay*	snack
la goyave *lah goh•yahv*	guava
la grenade *lah gruh•nahd*	pomegranate

la groseille *lah groh·zehy*	red currant
le hamburger *luh awN·bewr·gayr*	hamburger
le hareng *luh ah·rawN*	herring
les haricots *lay ah·ree·koh*	beans
les haricots verts *lay ah·ree·koh vehr*	green beans
le homard *luh oh·mahr*	lobster
le hot dog *luh oht dohg*	hot dog
l'huile d'olive *lweel doh·leev*	olive oil
l'huître *lwee·truh*	oyster
le jambon *luh zhawN·bohN*	ham
le jaune/blanc d'œuf *luh zhohn/ blawN duhf*	egg yolk/white
le jus *luh zhew*	juice
le ketchup *luh keht·shuhp*	ketchup
le kiwi *luh kee·wee*	kiwi
le lait *luh lay*	milk
le lait de soja *luh lait duh soh·zhah*	soya milk
la laitue *lah lay·tew*	lettuce
la langue *lah lawNg*	tongue
le lapin *luh lah·pehN*	rabbit
les légumes *lay lay·gewm*	vegetables
les lentilles *lay lawN·tee·yuh*	lentils
la limonade *lah lee·moh·nahd*	lemon soda
la liqueur d'oranges *lah lee·kuhr doh·rawNzh*	orange liqueur
la liqueur *lah lee·kuhr*	liqueur
les macaronis *lay mah·kah·roh·nee*	macaroni
le maïs *luh mah·ees*	sweet corn
la mandarine *lah mawN·dah·reen*	tangerine
la mangue *lah mawNg*	mango
le maquereau *luh mah·kuh·roh*	mackerel

la margarine *lah mahr·gah·reen*	margarine
la marmelade *lah mahr·muh·lahd*	marmalade
le marron *luh mah·rohN*	chestnut
la mayonnaise *lah mah·yohN·nehz*	mayonnaise
le melon *luh muh·lohN*	melon
la menthe *lah mawNt*	mint
la meringue *lah muh·rehNg*	meringue
le miel *luh meeyehl*	honey
la morue *lah moh·rew*	cod
les moules *lay mool*	mussels
la moutarde *lah moo·tahrd*	mustard
le mouton *luh moo·tohN*	mutton
la mûre *lah mewr*	blackberry
la myrtille *lah meer·teeyuh*	blueberry
le navet *luh nah·vay*	turnip
la noisette *lah nwah·zeht*	hazelnut
les noix *lay nwah*	nuts
la noix de cajou *lah nwah duh kah·zhoo*	cashew
la noix de coco *lah nwah duh koh·koh*	coconut
la noix de muscade *lah nwah duh mew·skahd*	nutmeg
la noix de pecan *lah nwah duh peh·kawN*	pecan
la nouille *lah noohy*	noodle
l'œuf *luhf*	egg
l'oie *lwah*	goose
l'oignon *loh·neeyohN*	onion
l'olive *loh·leev*	olive
l'omelette *loh·muh·leht*	omelet
l'orange *loh·rawNzh*	orange
l'orangeade *loh·rawN·zhad*	orange soda [squash]
l'origan *loh·ree·gawN*	oregano

le pain *luh pehN* — bread
le pain grillé *luh pehN gree·yay* — toast
les palourdes *lay pah·loord* — clams
le pamplemousse *luh pawN·pluh·moos* — grapefruit
le panais *luh pah·nay* — parsnip
la papaye *lah pah·pie* — papaya
la pastèque *lah pahs·tehk* — watermelon
la patate douce *lah pah·taht doos* — sweet potato
la pâte d'amande *lah paht dah·mawNd* — marzipan
le pâté *luh pah·tay* — pâté
les pâtes *lay paht* — pasta
les pâtisseries *lay pah·tee·suh·ree* — pastries
la pêche *lah pehsh* — peach
la perche *lah pehrsh* — sea perch
le persil *luh pehr·seel* — parsley
le petit pain *luh puh·tee pehN* — roll
les petits pois *lay puh·tee pwah* — peas
la pintade *lah pehN·tahd* — guinea fowl
la pizza *lah peed·zah* — pizza
les pois chiches *lay pwah sheesh* — chickpeas
la poire *lah pwahr* — pear

le poireau *luh pwah•roh*	leek
le poisson *luh pwah•sohN*	fish
le poivre *luh pwah•vruh*	black pepper
le piment *luh pee•mawN*	chili pepper
le poivron *luh pwah•vrohN*	pepper (vegetable)
le piment doux *luh pee•mawN doo*	sweet pepper
la pomme *lah pohm*	apple
la pomme de terre *lah pohm duh tehr*	potato
le porc *luh pohr*	pork
le porto *luh pohr•toh*	port
le potage *luh poh•tahzh*	stew
la poule *lah pool*	hen
le poulet *luh poo•lay*	chicken
le poulpe *luh poolp*	octopus
la prune *lah prewn*	plum
le pruneau *luh prew•noh*	prune
la queue de bœuf *lah kuh duh buhf*	oxtail
le radis *luh rah•dee*	radish
le raisin *luh reh•zehN*	grape
le raisin sec *luh reh•zehN sehk*	raisin
la rhubarbe *lah rew•bahrb*	rhubarb

le rhum *luh ruhm*	rum
le riz *luh ree*	rice
le rognon *luh roh•nyohN*	kidney
le romarin *luh roh•mah•rehN*	rosemary
le rôti *luh roh•tee*	roast
le rôti de bœuf *luh roh•tee duh buhf*	roast beef
le safran *luh sah•frawN*	saffron
la salade *lah sah•lahd*	salad
le sandwich *luh sawN•dweesh*	sandwich
la sardine *lah sahr•deen*	sardine
la sauce *lah sohs*	sauce
la sauce à l'ail *lah sohs ah lie*	garlic sauce
la sauce aigre douce	sweet and sour sauce
lah sohs eh•gruh doos	
la sauce piquante *lah sohs pee•kawNt*	hot pepper sauce
la sauce soja *lah sohs soh•zhah*	soy sauce
la saucisse *lah soh•sees*	sausage
le saucisson *luh soh•see•sohN*	salami
la sauge *lah sohzh*	sage
le saumon *luh soh•mohN*	salmon
la scarole *lah skah•rohl*	escarole [chicory]
le scotch *luh skoh•tsh*	scotch
le sel *luh sehl*	salt
le sherry *luh sheh•ree*	sherry
le sirop *luh see•roh*	syrup
le soda *luh soh•dah*	soda
le soja *luh soh•zhah*	soy [soya]/soybean [soya bean]
la sole *lah sohl*	sole
la soupe *lah soop*	soup
les spaghettis *lay spah•geh•tee*	spaghetti

les spiritueux *lay spee•ree•tewuh*	spirits
le steak *luh stayk*	steak
le sucre *luh sew•kruh*	sugar
les sucreries *lay sew•kreh•ree*	sweets
la tarte *lah tahrt*	pie
le thé *luh tay*	tea
le thon *luh tohN*	tuna
le thym *luh tehN*	thyme
le tofu *luh toh•few*	tofu
la tomate *lah toh•maht*	tomato
les tripes *lay treep*	tripe
la truffe *lah trewf*	truffle
la truite *lah trweet*	trout
la vanille *lah vah•neeyuh*	vanilla
le veau *luh voh*	veal
la venaison *lah vuh•neh•sohN*	venison
le vermouth *luh vehr•moot*	vermouth
la viande *lah veeyawNd*	meat
le vin *luh vehN*	wine
le vin de dessert *luh vehN duh day•sehr*	dessert wine
le vinaigre *luh vee•neh•gruh*	vinegar

la vodka *lah vohd•kah* vodka
la volaille *lah voh•lie* poultry
le whisky *luh wees•kee* whisky
le yaourt *luh yah•oort* yogurt

People

Conversation 103

Romance 109

ESSENTIAL

Hello!/Hi!	**Bonjour !/Salut !**	*bohN·zhoor/sah·lew*
How are you?	**Comment allez-vous ?**	*koh·mawN tah·lay·voo*
Fine, thanks.	**Bien, merci.**	*beeyehN mehr·see*
Excuse me!	**Excusez-moi !**	*ehk·skew·zay·mwah*
Do you speak English?	**Parlez-vous anglais ?**	*pahr·lay·voo zawN·glay*
What's your name?	**Comment vous appelez-vous ?** *koh·mawN voo zah·puh·lay·voo*	
My name is…	**Je m'appelle…** *zhuh mah·pehl…*	
Nice to meet you.	**Enchanté** *m* /**Enchantée** *f.* *awN·shawN·tay*	
Where are you from?	**D'où êtes-vous ?** *doo eht·voo*	
I'm from the U.K./U.S.	**Je viens du Royaume-Uni/des États-Unis.** *zhuh veeyehN dew rwah·yohm·ew·nee/day zay·tah·zew·nee*	
What do you do for a living?	**Que faites-vous dans la vie ?** *kuh feht·voo dawN lah vee*	
I work for…	**Je travaille pour…** *zhuh trah·vie poor…*	
I'm a student.	**Je suis étudiant** *m* /**étudiante** *f.* *zhuh swee zay·tew·deeyawN / zay·tew·deeyawnt*	
I'm retired.	**Je suis à la retraite.** *zhuh swee zah lah ruh·trayt*	
Do you like…?	**Aimez-vous…?** *eh·may·voo…*	
Goodbye.	**Au revôir.** *oh ruh·vwahr*	
See you later.	**À bientôt.** *ah beeyehN·toh*	

When addressing someone, it is polite to include a title: **monsieur** for a man or **madame** for a woman, even if you suspect she is not married. **Mademoiselle** is used only when addressing young girls.

Language Difficulties

Do you speak English?	**Parlez-vous anglais ?** *pahr·lay·voo zawN·glay*
Does anyone here speak English?	**Est-ce que quelqu'un parle anglais ici ?** *ehs kuh kehl·kuhN pahrl awN·glay ee·see*
I don't speak (much) French.	**Je ne parle pas (bien le) français.** *zhuh nuh pahrl pah (beeyehN luh) frawN·say*
Can you speak more slowly?	**Pouvez-vous parler plus lentement ?** *poo·vay·voo pahr·lay plew lawN·tuh·mawN*
Can you repeat that?	**Pouvez-vous répéter ?** *poo·vay·voo ray·pay·tay*
Excuse me?	**Excusez-moi ?** *ehk·skew·zay·mwah*
Can you spell it?	**Pouvez-vous l'épeler ?** *poo·vay·voo lay·puh·lay*
Can you write it down?	**S'il vous plaît, écrivez-le.** *seel voo play ay·kree·vay·luh*
Can you translate this into English for me?	**Pouvez-vous traduire ceci en anglais pour moi ?** *poo·vay·voo trah·dweer suh·see awN nawN·glay poor mwah*
What does this/that mean?	**Qu'est ce que ceci/cela veut dire ?** *kehs kuh suh·see/suh·lah vuh deer*
I understand.	**Je comprends.** *zhuh kohN·prawN*
I don't understand.	**Je ne comprends pas.** *zhuh nuh kohN·prawN pah*
Do you understand?	**Comprenez-vous ?** *kohN·pruh·nay·voo*

YOU MAY HEAR...

Je parle un peu anglais.
zhuh pahrl uhN puh awN·glay

I only speak a little English.

Je ne parle pas anglais.
zhuh nuh pahrl pah zawN·glay

I don't speak English.

Making Friends

Hello!	**Bonjour !** *bohN·zhoor*
Good afternoon.	**Bon après-midi.** *bohN nah·pray·mee·dee*
Good evening.	**Bonsoir.** *bohN·swahr*
My name is...	**Je m'appelle...** *zhuh mah·pehl...*
What's your name?	**Comment vous appelez-vous ?** *koh·mawN voo zah·puh·lay·voo*
I'd like to introduce you to...	**Je voudrais vous présenter...** *zhuh voo·dray voo pray·zawN·tay...*
Pleased to meet you.	**Enchanté** *m* / **Enchantée** *f.* *awN·shawN·tay*
How are you?	**Comment allez-vous ?** *koh·mawN tah·lay·voo*
Fine, thanks. And you?	**Bien, merci. Et vous ?** *beeyehN mehr·see ay voo*

In France, people greet each other with a firm handshake on first meeting. Once they become more familiar, people give from one to four or more kisses (cheek-to-cheek contact). Cheek-kissing among men, however, is usually reserved for family members and close friends.

Travel Talk

I'm here…	**Je suis ici…** *zhuh swee zee•see…*
on business	**pour les affaires** *poor lay zah•fehr*
on vacation [holiday]	**en vacances** *awN vah•kawNs*
studying	**pour étudier** *poor ay•tew•deeyay*
I'm staying for…	**Je reste pour…** *zhuh rehst poor…*
I've been here…	**Je suis ici depuis…** *zhuh swee zee•see duh•pwee…*
a day	**un jour** *uhN zhoor*
a week	**une semaine** *ewn suh•mehN*
a month	**un mois** *uhN mwah*
Where are you from?	**D'où êtes-vous ?** *doo eht•voo*
I'm from…	**Je suis de…** *zhuh swee duh…*

Personal

Who are you with?	**Avec qui êtes-vous ?** *ah•vehk kee eht•voo*
I'm here alone.	**Je suis seul *m*/seule *f*.** *zhuh swee suhl*
I'm with…	**Je suis avec…** *zhuh swee zah•vehk…*
my husband/wife	**mon mari *m*/ma femme *f*.** *mohN mah•ree/mah fahm*

my boyfriend/	**mon petit-ami** *m* **/ma petite-amie** *f*
girlfriend	*mawN puh•tee•tah•mee /mah puh•tee•tah•mee*
a friend	**un ami** *m* **/une amie** *f*
	uhN nah•mee /ewn ah•mee
friends	**des amis** *day zah•mee*
a colleague	**un collègue** *m* **/une collègue** *f*
	uhN koh•lehg /ewn koh•lehg
colleagues	**des collègues** *day koh•lehg*
When's your	**Quand est votre anniversaire ?**
birthday?	*kawN teh voh•truh ah•nee•vehr•sehr*
How old are you?	**Quel âge avez-vous ?** *keh lahzh ah•vay•voo*
I'm…	**J'ai…ans.** *zhay…awN*
Are you married?	**Êtes-vous marié** *m* **/mariée** *f* **?**
	eht•voo mah•reeyay
I'm…	**Je suis…** *zhuh swee…*
single/in a	**célibataire/en ménage**
relationship	*say•lee•bah•tehr/ awN may•nahzh*
engaged	**fiancé** *m* **/fiancée** *f* *feeyawN•say*
married	**marié** *m* **/mariée** *f* *mah•reeyay*
divorced	**divorcé** *m* **/divorcée** *f* *dee•vohr•say*
separated	**séparé** *m* **/séparée** *f* *say•pah•ray*
widowed	**veuf** *m* **/veuve** *f* *vuhf /vuhv*
Do you have children/	**Avez-vous des enfants/petits-enfants ?**
grandchildren ?	*ah•vay•voo day zawN•fawN/*
	puh•tee•zawN•fawN

For Numbers, see page 173.

Work & School

What do you do for a living?	**Que faites-vous dans la vie ?** *kuh feht•voo dawN lah vee*
What are you studying?	**Qu'étudiez-vous ?** *kay•tew•deeyay•voo*
I'm studying French.	**J'étudie le français.** *zhay•tew•dee luh frawN•say*
I...	**Je...** *zhuh...*
work full-/part-time	**travaille à temps plein/partiel** *trah•vie ah tawN plehN/pahr•syehl*
am unemployed	**suis au chômage** *swee zoh shoh•mahzh*
work at home	**travaille à la maison** *trah•vie ah lah may•zohN*
Who do you work for?	**Pour qui travaillez-vous ?** *poor kee trah•vie•yay•voo*
I work for...	**Je travaille pour...** *zhuh trah•vie poor...*
Here's my business card.	**Voici ma carte de visite.** *vwah•see mah kahrt duh vee•zeet*

For Business Travel, see page 145.

Weather

What's the forecast?	**Que dit la météo ?** *kuh dee lah may•tay•oh*
What beautiful/terrible weather!	**Quel beau/terrible temps !** *kehl boh/teh•ree•bluh tawN*
It's...	**Il fait...** *Eel fay...*
cool/warm	**frais/chaud** *fray/shoh*
cold/hot	**froid/très chaud** *frwah/tray shoh*
rainy/sunny	**pluvieux/ensoleillé** *plew•veeyuh/awN•soh•lehyay*
snowy/icy	**enneigé/gelé** *awN•neh•zhay/zheh•lay*
Do I need a jacket/an umbrella ?	**Ai-je besoin d'une veste/d'un parapluie ?** *ay•zhuh buh•zwehN dewn vehst/duhN pah•rah•plewee*

For Temperature, see page 179.

Romance

ESSENTIAL

Would you like to go out for a drink/dinner?	**Voudriez-vous aller prendre un verre/ sortir dîner?** voo•dreeyay•voo ah•lay prawN•druh uhN vehr/sohr•teer dee•nay
What are your plans for tonight/ tomorrow?	**Quels sont vos projets pour ce soir/ demain?** kehl sohN voh proh•zhay poor suh swahr/duh•mehN
Can I have your (phone) number?	**Puis-je avoir votre numéro (de téléphone)?** pwee•zhuh ah•vwahr voh•truh new•may•roh (duh tay•lay•fohn)
Can I join you?	**Puis-je me joindre à vous?** pwee•zhuh muh zhwehN•druh ah voo
Can I buy you a drink?	**Puis-je vous offrir un verre?** pwee•zhuh voo zoh•freer uhN vehr
I love you.	**Je t'aime.** zhuh tehm

The Dating Game

Would you like to go out…?	**Voudriez-vous sortir…?** voo•dreeyay•voo sohr•teer…
for coffee	**prendre un café** prawN•druh uhN kah•fay
for a drink	**prendre un verre** prawN•druh uhN vehr
to dinner	**aller dîner** ah•lay dee•nay
What are your plans for…?	**Quels sont vos projets pour…?** kehl sohN voh proh•zhay poor…
today	**aujourd'hui** oh•zhoor•dwee
tonight	**ce soir** suh swahr
tomorrow	**demain** duh•mehN
this weekend	**ce weekend** suh wee•kehnd

Where would you like to go?	**Où voudriez-vous aller ?**
	oo voo-dreeyay-voo ah-lay
I'd like to go to…	**Je voudrais aller à…**
	zhuh voo-dray ah-lay ah…
Do you like…?	**Aimez-vous…?** *eh-may-voo…*
Can I have your phone number/ e-mail ?	**Puis-je avoir votre numero de téléphone/ mail ?** *pwee-zhuh ah-vwahr voh-truh new-may-roh duh tay-lay-fohn/mehyl*
Are you on Facebook /Twitter?	**Êtes-vous sur Facebook/Twitter ?** *eht-voo sewr fayhs-book/twee-teuhr*
Can I join you?	**Puis-je me joindre à vous ?** *pwee-zhuh muh zhwehN-druh ah voo*
You're very attractive.	**Vous êtes très beau *m* /belle *f*.** *voo zeht tray boh/behl*
Let's go somewhere quieter.	**Allons dans un endroit plus calme.** *ah-lohN dawN zuhN nawN-drwah plew kahlm*

For Communications, see page 48.

Accepting & Rejecting

I'd love to.	**Avec plaisir.** *ah-vehk play-zeer*
Where should we meet?	**Où devons-nous nous retrouver ?** *oo duh-vohN-noo noo ruh-troo-vay*
I'll meet you at the bar/your hotel.	**Je vous retrouverai au bar/à votre hôtel.** *zhuh voo ruh-troo-vuh-ray oh bahr/ah voh-truh oh-tehl*
I'll come by at…	**Je viendrai à…** *zhuh veeyehN-dray ah…*
I'm busy.	**Je suis occupé *m* /occupée *f*.** *zhuh swee zoh-kew-pay*
I'm not interested.	**Je ne suis pas intéressé *m* /intéressée *f*.** *zhuh nuh swee pah ehN-tay-reh-say*

| Leave me alone. | **Laissez-moi tranquille.** *leh·say mwah trawN·keel* |
| Stop bothering me! | **Fichez-moi la paix !** *fee·shay·mwah lah pay* |

Getting Intimate

Can I hug/kiss you?	**Puis-je vous enlacer/embrasser ?**
	pwee·zhuh voo zawN·lah·say/zawN·brah·say
Yes.	**Oui.** *wee*
No.	**Non.** *nohN*
Stop!	**Arrêtez !** *ah·reh·tay*
I love you.	**Je t'aime.** *zhuh tehm*

Sexual Preferences

Are you gay?	**Êtes-vous gay ?** *eht·voo gay*
I'm…	**Je suis…** *zhuh swee…*
heterosexual	**hétérosexuel** *m* **/hétérosexuelle** *f*
	ay·tay·roh·sehk·sewehl
homosexual	**homosexuel** *m* **/homosexuelle** *f*
	oh·moh·sehk·sewehl
bisexual	**bisexuel** *m* **/bisexuelle** *f* *bee·sehk·sewehl*
Do you like	**Aimez-vous les hommes/femmes ?**
men/women ?	*ay·may·voo lay zohm/fahm*

Leisure Time

Sightseeing   113
Shopping   117
Sport & Leisure   134
Going Out   141

Sightseeing

ESSENTIAL

Where's the tourist information office?	**Où est l'office de tourisme ?** *oo ay loh•fees duh too•ree•smuh*
What are the main sights?	**Quelles sont les choses importantes à voir ?** *kehl sohN lay shoh zehN•pohr•tawN tah vwahr*
Do you offer tours in English?	**Proposez-vous des visites en anglais ?** *Proh•poh•zay•voo day vee•zeet awN nawN•glay*
Can I have a map/guide?	**Puis-je avoir une carte/un guide ?** *pwee•zhuh ah•vwahr ewn kahrt/uhN geed*

Tourist Information

Do you have information on...?	**Avez-vous des renseignements sur...?** *ah•vay•voo day rawN•seh•nyuh•mawN sewr...*
Can you recommend...?	**Pouvez-vous me conseiller...?** *poo•vay•voo muh kohN•say•yay...*
a bus tour	**une visite en bus** *ewn vee•zeet awN bews*
an excursion to...	**une excursion pour...** *ewn ehk•skewr•seeyohN poor...*
a sightseeing tour of...	**une visite de...** *ewn vee•zeet duh...*

Offices de tourisme or **syndicats d'initiative** (tourism offices) are usually located near the downtown area, next to train stations or close to city hall. They can provide a wealth of information about lodging, entertainment, restaurants, etc.

On Tour

I'd like to go on the excursion to…	**Je voudrais faire cette excursion à…** *zhuh voo•dray fehr seh tehk•skewr•seeyohN nah…*
When's the next tour?	**Quand a lieu la prochaine visite ?** *kawN tah leeyuh lah proh•shehn vee•zeet*
Are there tours in English?	**Y-a-t-il des visites en anglais ?** *yah•teel day vee•zeet zawN nawN•glay*
Is there an English guide book/audio guide?	**Y-a-t-il un guide/audio guide en anglais ?** *yah•teel uhN geed/oh•deeyoh geed awN nawN•glay*
What time do we leave/return?	**À quelle heure partons-nous/revenons-nous ?** *ah keh luhr pahr•tohN•noo/ruh•vuh•nohN•noo*
We'd like to see…	**Nous voudrions voir…** *noo voo•dreeyohN vwahr…*
Can we stop here…?	**Pouvons-nous nous arrêter ici pour…?** *poo•vohN•noo noo zah•reh•tay ee•see poor…*
to take photos	**prendre des photos** *prawN•druh day foh•toh*
for souvenirs	**acheter des souvenirs** *ah•shtay day soo•vuh•neer*
for the toilets	**aller aux toilettes** *ah•lay oh twah•leht*
Is it disabled-accessible?	**Est-ce que c'est accessible aux handicapés ?** *ehs kuh say tahk•say•see•bluh oh zawN•dee•kah•pay*

For Tickets, see page 18.

Seeing the Sights

Where's…?	**Où est…?** *oo ay…*
the battleground	**le champ de bataille** *luh shawN duh bah•tie*
the botanical	**le jardin botanique**

garden	*luh zhahr•dehN boh•tah•neek*
the castle	**le château** *luh shah•toh*
the downtown area	**le centre-ville** *luh sawN•truh•veel*
the fountain	**la fontaine** *lah fohN•tehn*
the library	**la bibliothèque** *lah bee•bleeyoh•tehk*
the market	**le marché** *luh mahr•shay*
the museum	**le musée** *luh mew•zay*
the old town	**la vieille ville** *lah veeyeh•yuh veel*
the opera house	**l'opéra** *loh•pay•rah*
the palace	**le palais** *luh pah•lay*
the park	**le parc** *luh pahrk*
the ruins	**les ruines** *lay rween*
the shopping area	**le quartier commercial** *luh kahr•teeyay koh•mehr•seeyahl*
the town square	**la grand-place** *lah grawN•plahs*
Can you show me on the map?	**Pouvez-vous me montrer sur la carte ?** *poo•vay-voo muh mohN•tray sewr lah kahrt*
It's…	**C'est…** *say…*
amazing	**surprenant** *sewr•preh•nawN*
beautiful	**beau** *boh*

boring	**ennuyeux**	*awN·nwee·yuh*
interesting	**intéressant**	*ehN·tay·reh·sawN*
magnificent	**magnifique**	*mah·nee·feek*
romantic	**romantique**	*roh·mawN·teek*
strange	**étrange**	*ay·trawNzh*
terrible	**terrible**	*teh·ree·bluh*
ugly	**laid**	*lay*
I (don't) like it.	**Je (n')aime (pas).**	*zhuh (n)ehm (pah)*

For Asking Directions, see page 33.

Religious Sites

Where's…?	**Où est…?**	*oo ay…*
the cathedral	**la cathédrale**	*lah kah·tay·drahl*
the Catholic/ Protestant church	**l'église catholique/protestante** *lay·gleez kah·toh·leek/proh·tehs·tawNt*	
the mosque	**la mosquée**	*lah mohs·kay*
the shrine	**le lieu saint**	*luh leeyuh sehN*
the synagogue	**la synagogue**	*lah see·nah·gohg*
the temple	**le temple**	*luh tawN·pluh*
What time is the service?	**À quelle heure est la messe ?** *ah keh luhr ay lah mehs*	

ESSENTIAL

Where's the market/ mall	**Où est le marché/centre commercial ?** *oo ay luh mahr·shay/sawN·truh koh·mehr·seeyahl*
I'm just looking.	**Je regarde seulement.** *zhuh ruh·gahrd suhl·mawN*
Can you help me?	**Pouvez-vous m'aider ?** *poo·vay·voo meh·day*
I'm being helped.	**On s'occupe de moi.** *ohN soh·kewp duh mwah*
How much?	**Combien ça coûte ?** *kohN·beeyehN sah koot*
That one, please.	**Celui-ci** *m* **/Celle-ci** *f* **, s'il vous plaît.** *suh·lwee·see/sehl see seel voo play*
That's all.	**C'est tout.** *say too*
Where can I pay?	**Où puis-je payer ?** *oo pwee·zhuh pay·yay*
I'll pay in cash/by credit card.	**Je paierai en espèces/par carte de crédit.** *zhuh pay·ray awN neh·spehs/pahr kahrt duh kray·dee*
A receipt, please.	**Un reçu, s'il vous plaît.** *uhN ruh·sew seel voo play*

At the Shops

Where's…?	**Où est…** *oo ay…*
the antiques store	**l'antiquaire** *lawN·tee·kehr*
the bakery	**la boulangerie** *lah boo·lawN·zhuh·ree*
the bank	**la banque** *lah bawNk*
the bookstore	**la librairie** *lah lee·breh·ree*
the clothing store	**le magasin de vêtements** *luh mah·gah·zehN duh veht·mawN*
the delicatessen	**la charcuterie** *lah shar·kew·tuh·ree*
the department store	**le grand magasin** *luh grawN mah·gah·zehN*

the gift shop	**la boutique cadeaux** *lah boo-teek kah-doh*
the health food store	**le magasin de diététique** *luh mah-gah-zehN duh deeyay-tay-teek*
the jeweler	**la bijouterie** *lah bee-zhoo-tuh-ree*
the liquor store [off-licence]	**le marchand de vins et de spiritueux** *luh mahr-shawN duh vehN ay duh spee-ree-tewuh*
the market	**le marché** *luh mahr-shay*
the music store	**le disquaire** *luh dees-kehr*
the pastry shop	**la pâtisserie** *lah pah-tee-suh-ree*
the pharmacy	**la pharmacie** *lah fahr-mah-see*
the produce [grocery] store	**le magasin de fruits et légumes** *luh mah-gah-zehN duh frwee zay lay-gewm*
the shoe store	**le magasin de chaussures** *luh mah-gah-zehN duh shoh-sewr*
the shopping mall	**le centre commercial** *luh sawN-truh koh-mehr-seeyahl*
the souvenir store	**le magasin de souvenirs** *luh mah-gah-zehN duh soo-vuh-neer*
the supermarket	**le supermarché** *luh sew-pehr-mahr-shay*
the tobacconist	**le bureau de tabac** *luh bew-roh duh tah-bahk*
the toy store	**le magasin de jouets** *luh mah-gah-zehN duh zhooway*

Ask an Assistant

When do you open/close?	**À quelle heure ouvrez-vous/fermez-vous ?** *ah kehl uhr oo-vray-voo/fehr-may-voo*
Where's…?	**Où est…?** *oo ay…*
the cashier	**la caisse** *lah kehs*
the escalator	**l'escalator** *lehs-kah-lah-tohr*
the elevator [lift]	**l'ascenseur** *lah-sawN-suhr*
the fitting room	**la cabine d'essayage** *lah kah-been deh-say-yahzh*

the store directory	**le plan du magasin** *luh plawN dewmah•gah•zehN*
Can you help me?	**Pouvez-vous m'aider ?** *poo•vay•voo meh•day*
I'm just looking.	**Je regarde seulement.** *zhuh ruh•gahrd suhl•mawN*
I'm being helped.	**On s'occupe de moi.** *ohN soh•kewp duh mwah*
Do you have…?	**Avez-vous…?** *ah•vay•voo…*
Can you show me…?	**Pouvez-vous me montrer…?** *poo•vay•voo muh mohN•tray…*
Can you ship/wrap it?	**Pouvez-vous le livrer/l'emballer ?** *poo•vay•voo luh lee•vray/lawN•bah•lay*
How much?	**Combien ça coûte ?** *kohN•beeyehN sah koot*
That's all.	**C'est tout.** *say too*

For Clothing, see page 125.
For Meals & Cooking, see page 67.
For Souvenirs, see page 132.

YOU MAY HEAR…

Je peux vous aider ? *zhuh puh voo zeh•day*	Can I help you?
Un instant. *uhN nehNs•tawN*	One moment.
Que désirez-vous ? *kuh day•zee•ray•voo*	What would you like?
Autre chose ? *oh•truh shohz*	Anything else?

YOU MAY SEE...

OUVERT/FERMÉ	open/closed
FERMÉ POUR LE DÉJEUNER	closed for lunch
CABINE D'ESSAYAGE	fitting room
CAISSE	cashier
ESPÈCES SEULEMENT	cash only
CARTES ACCEPTÉES	credit cards accepted
HEURES D'OUVERTURE	business hours
SORTIE	exit

Personal Preferences

I'd like something...	**Je voudrais quelque chose...**
	zhuh voo•dray kehl•kuh shohz...
cheap/expensive	**de bon marché/cher** *duh bohN mahr•shay/shehr*
larger/smaller	**de plus grand/petit** *duh plew grawN/puh•tee*
from this region	**de cette région** *duh seht ray•zheeyohN*
Around...euros.	**Pour à peu près...euros.**
	poor ah puh pray...uh•roh
Is it real?	**Est-ce que c'est du vrai ?** *ehs kuh say dew vray*
Can you show me	**Pouvez-vous me montrer ceci/cela ?**
this/that?	*poo•vay-voo muh mohN•tray suh•see/suh•lah*
That's not quite	**Ce n'est pas exactement ce que je veux.**
what I want.	*suh nay pah zehk•sahk•tuh•mawN suh kuh zhuh vuh*
No, I don't like it.	**Non, je n'aime pas.** *nohN zhuh nehm pah*
It's too expensive.	**C'est trop cher.** *say troh shehr*
I have to think about it.	**Je dois réfléchir.** *zhuh dwah ray•flay•sheer*
I'll take it.	**Je le *m* /la *f* prends.** *zhuh luh /lah prawN*

Paying & Bargaining

How much?	**Combien ça fait ?** *kohN‑beeyehN sah fay*
I'll pay...	**Je paierai...** *zhuh pay‑ray...*
in cash	**en espèces** *awN nehs‑pehs*
by credit card	**par carte de crédit** *pahr kahrt duh kray‑dee*
by traveller's cheque	**avec des chèques de voyages** *ah‑vehk day shehk duh vwah‑yahzh*
A receipt, please.	**Un reçu, s'il vous plaît.** *uhN ruh‑sew seel voo play*
That's too much.	**C'est beaucoup trop.** *say boh‑koo troh*
I'll give you...	**Je vous en propose...** *zhuh voo zawN proh‑pohz...*
I have only...euros.	**Je n'ai que...euros.** *zhuh nay kuh...uh‑roh*
Is that your best price?	**Est‑ce que c'est votre meilleur prix ?** *ehs kuh say voh‑truh mehy‑yuhr pree*
Can you give me a discount?	**Pouvez‑vous me faire une remise ?** *poo‑vay‑voo muh fehr ewn ruh‑meez*

For Numbers, see page 173.

Cash (the euro) is always accepted. Credit and debit cards can be used in cash machines and for purchases. Check with your bank before leaving to obtain a PIN for both debit and credit cards; you'll usually be asked to enter your PIN instead of signing when making purchases. Traveler's checks are also widely accepted in France.

YOU MAY HEAR...

Comment voulez-vous payer ?	How are you paying?
koh·mawN voo·lay·voo pay·yay	
Votre carte de crédit est refusée.	Your credit card has
voh·truh kahrt duh kray·dee tay ruh·few·zay	been declined.
Une pièce d'identité, s'il vous plaît.	ID, please.
ewn peeyehs dee·dawN·tee·tay seel voo play	
Nous n'acceptons pas les cartes de crédit.	We don't accept
noo nahk·sehp·tohN pah lay kahrt duh kray·dee	credit cards.
En espèces seulement, s'il vous plaît.	Cash only, please.
awN nehs·pehs suhl·mawN seel voo play	

Making a Complaint

I'd like...	**Je voudrais...** *zhuh voo·dray...*
to exchange this	**échanger ceci** *ay·shawN·zhay suh·see*
a refund	**un remboursement**
	uhN rawN·boor·suh·mawN
to see the manager	**voir le responsable**
	vwahr luh rehs·pohN·sah·bluh

Services

Can you recommend…?	**Pouvez-vous me conseiller…?** *poo•vay•voo muh kohN•say•yay…*
a barber	**un coiffeur pour hommes** *uhN kwah•fuhr poor ohm*
a dry cleaner	**une teinturerie** *ewn tehN•tewr•ree*
a laundromat [launderette]	**une laverie automatique** *ewn lah•vuh•reeoh•toh•mah•teek*
a nail salon	**une onglerie** *ewn ohN•gluh•ree*
a spa	**une station de balnéothérapie** *ewn stah•seeyohN duh bahl•nayoh•tay•rah•pee*
a travel agency	**une agence de voyage** *ewn ah•zhawNs duh vwah•yahzh*
Can you…this?	**Pouvez-vous…ceci ?** *poo•vay•voo…suh•see*
alter	**changer** *shawN•zhay*
clean	**nettoyer** *neh•twah•yay*
fix	**raccourcir** *rah•koor•seer*
press	**repasser** *ruh•pah•say*
When will it be ready?	**Quand cela sera-t-il prêt ?** *kawN suh•lah seh•rah•teel preh*

Hair & Beauty

I'd like…	**Je voudrais…** *zhuh voo•dray…*
an appointment for today/tomorrow	**un rendez-vous pour aujourd'hui/ demain** *uhN rawN•day•voo poor oh•zhoor•dwee/duh•mehN*
some color/ highlights	**une couleur/des mèches** *ewn koo•luhr/day mehsh*
my hair styled/	**une mise en forme/un brushing** *ewn mee zawN fohrm/uhN bruh•sheeng*
a haircut	**une coupe** *ewn koop*

an eyebrow/ bikini wax	**une épilation à la cire des sourcils/du maillot** *ewn ay•pee•lah•seeyohN nah lah seer* *day soor•seel/dew mieyoh*
a facial	**un soin du visage** *uhN swehN dew vee•zahzh*
a manicure/ pedicure	**une manucure/pédicure** *ewn pedicure mah•new•kewr/pay•dee•kewr*
a (sports) massage	**un massage (sportif)** *uhN mah•sahzh* *(spohr•teef)*
A trim, please.	**Égalisez les pointes, s'il vous plaît.** *ay•gah•lee•zay lay pwehNt seel voo play*
Not too short.	**Pas trop court.** *pah troh koor*
Shorter here.	**Plus court ici.** *plew koor ee•see*
Do you offer…?	**Proposez-vous…?** *proh•poh•zay•voo…*
acupuncture	**de l'acupuncture** *duh lah•kew•pohNk•tewr*
aromatherapy	**de l'aromathérapie** *duh lah•roh•mah•tay•rah•pee*
oxygen treatment	**des soins à l'oxygène** *day swehN ahlohk•see•zhehn*
a sauna	**un sauna** *uhN soh•nah*

Les stations de balnéothérapie (spas) are popular in France; day spas, especially, can be found in Paris and along the French Riviera. Many villages and resorts specialize in water therapies. The hot springs at Dax have been popular since Roman times, and the town is still one of France's most popular spa destinations. Some spas in the Bordeaux region specialize in wine-based therapies. In addition to the therapies, spa towns may also offer beautiful scenery, casinos, restaurants and outdoor activities.

Antiques

How old is it?	**De quand date-t-il *m* /date-elle *f* ?**
	duh kawN dah·teel/dah·tehl
Do you have	**Avez-vous quelque chose de la période…?**
anything from	*ah·vay·voo kehl·kuh shohz duh lah pay·reeyohd…*
the…period?	
Do I have to fill	**Dois-je remplir des formulaires ?**
out any forms?	*dwah·zhuh rawN·pleer day fohr·mew·lehr*
Is there a certificate	**Y-a-t-il un certificat d'authenticité ?**
of authenticity?	*yah·teel uhN sehr·tee·fee·kah doh·tawN·tee·see·tay*
Can you ship/	**Pouvez-vous le livrer/l'emballer ?**
wrap it?	*poo·vay·voo luh lee·vray/lawN·bah·lay*

Clothing

I'd like…	**Je voudrais…** *zhuh voo·dray…*
Can I try this on?	**Puis-je essayer ceci ?**
	pwee·zhuh eh·say·yay suh·see
It doesn't fit.	**Ça ne va pas.** *sah nuh vah pah*
It's too…	**C'est trop…** *say troh…*
big/small	**grand/petit** *grawN/puh·tee*
short/long	**court/long** *koor/lohng*

tight/loose	**serré/large** *seh•ray/lahrzh*
Do you have this in size…?	**Avez-vous ceci en taille…?** *ah•vay•voo suh•see awN tie…*
Do you have this in a bigger/smaller size?	**Avez-vous ceci en plus grand/petit ?** *ah•vay•voo suh•see awN plew grawN/puh•tee*

For Numbers, see page 173.

YOU MAY HEAR…

Ça vous va très bien. *sah voo vah tray beeyehN*	That looks great on you.
Comment ça me va ? *koh•mawN sah muh vah*	How does it fit?
Nous n'avons pas votre taille. *noo nah•vohN pah voh•truh tie*	We don't have your size.

Haute couture (designer fashion) and **prêt-à-porter** (ready-to-wear) boutiques can be found throughout Paris. The latest fashions by Dior®, Givenchy®, Saint-Laurent®, Chanel®, Jean-Paul Gaultier®, Ungaro®, Feraud®, Yamamoto® and Hermès® can be found in Paris well before making it to the U.S. or the U.K. Airport boutiques offer tax-free shopping and may have cheaper prices but fewer selections.

YOU MAY SEE…

HOMMES	men's
FEMMES	women's
ENFANTS	children's

Colors

I'd like something…	**Je voudrais quelque chose de…**
	zhuh voo•dray kehl•kuh shohz duh…
beige	**beige** *behzh*
black	**noir** *nwahr*
blue	**bleu** *bluh*
brown	**marron** *mah•rohN*
green	**vert** *vehr*
gray	**gris** *gree*
orange	**orange** *oh•rawNzh*
pink	**rose** *rohz*
purple	**violet** *veeyoh•lay*
red	**rouge** *roozh*
white	**blanc** *blawN*
yellow	**jaune** *zhohn*

Clothes & Accessories

a backpack	**un sac à dos** *uhN sahk ah doh*
a belt	**une ceinture** *ewn sehN•tewr*
a bikini	**un bikini** *uhN bee•kee•nee*
a blouse	**un chemisier** *uhN shuh•mee•zeeyay*

a bra	**un soutien-gorge** *uhN soo•teeyehN•gohrzh*
briefs [underpants]/ panties	**des slips/des culottes** *day sleep/day kew•loht*
a coat	**un manteau** *uhN mawN•toh*
a dress	**une robe** *ewn rohb*
a hat	**un chapeau** *uhN shah•poh*
a jacket	**une veste** *ewn vehst*
jeans	**un jean** *uhN zheen*
pajamas	**un pyjama** *uhN pee•zhah•mah*
pants [trousers]	**un pantalon** *uhN pawN•tah•lohN*
pantyhose [tights]	**un collant** *uhN koh•lawN*
a purse [handbag]	**un sac à main** *uhN sahk ah mehN*
a raincoat	**un imperméable** *uhN nehN•pehr•may•ah•bluh*
a scarf	**une écharpe** *ewn ay•sharp*
a shirt	**une chemise** *ewn shuh•meez*
shorts	**un short** *unN shohrt*
a skirt	**une jupe** *ewn zhewp*
socks	**des chaussettes** *day shoh•seht*
a suit	**un costume** *uhN kohs•tewm*
sunglasses	**des lunettes** *day lew•neht*
a sweater	**un pull** *uhN pewl*

a sweatshirt	**un sweat-shirt** *uhN sweht·shuhrt*
a swimsuit	**un maillot de bain** *uhN mie·yoh duh behN*
a T-shirt	**un t-shirt** *uhN tee·shuhrt*
a tie	**une cravate** *ewn krah·vaht*
underwear	**un sous-vêtement** *uhN soo·veht·mawN*

Fabric

I'd like...	**Je voudrais...** *zhuh voo·dray...*
cotton	**du coton** *dew koh·tohN*
denim	**du jean** *dew zheen*
lace	**de la dentelle** *duh lah dawN·tehl*
leather	**du cuir** *dew kweer*
linen	**du lin** *dew lehN*
silk	**de la soie** *duh lah swah*
wool	**de la laine** *duh lah lehn*
Is it machine washable?	**Est-ce lavable en machine ?** *ehs lah·vah·bluh awN mah·sheen*

Shoes

I'd like...	**Je voudrais...** *zhuh voo·dray...*
high-heels/flats	**des talons hauts/plats** *day tah·lohN oh/plah*
boots	**des bottes** *day boht*
loafers	**des mocassins** *day moh·kah·sehN*
sandals	**des sandales** *day sawN·dahl*
shoes	**des chaussures** *day shoh·sewr*
slippers	**des chaussons** *day shoh·sohN*
sneakers	**des tennis** *day tay·nees*
Size...	**Taille...** *tie...*

For Numbers, see page 173.

Sizes

small (S)	**petit** *puh·tee*
medium (M)	**moyen** *mwah·yawN*
large (L)	**grand** *grawN*
extra large (XL)	**très grand** *tray grawN*
petite	**menue** *muh·new*
plus size	**grande taille** *grawNd tie*

Newsagent & Tobacconist

Do you sell English-language newspapers?	**Vendez-vous des journaux en anglais ?** *vawN·day·voo day zhoor·noh awN nawN·glay*
I'd like...	**Je voudrais...** *zhuh voo·dray...*
candy [sweets]	**des bonbons** *day bohN·bohN*
chewing gum	**du chewing gum** *dew shew·weeng guhm*
a chocolate bar	**une barre de chocolat** *ewn bahr duh shoh·koh·lah*
a cigar	**un cigare** *uhN see·gahr*
a pack/carton of cigarettes	**un pack/une cartouche de cigarettes** *uhN pahk/ewn kahr·toosh duh see·gah·reht*
a lighter	**un briquet** *uhN bree·kay*
a magazine	**un magazine** *uhN mah·gah·zeen*
matches	**des allumettes** *day zah·lew·meht*
a newspaper	**un journal** *uhN zhoor·nahl*
a pen	**un stylo** *uhN stee·loh*
a postcard	**une carte postale** *ewn kahrt pohs·tahl*
a road/town map of...	**une carte routière/de la ville de...** *ewn kahrt roo·teeyehr/duh lah veel duh...*
stamps	**des timbres** *day tehN·bruh*

You can find many English-language newspapers at newsstands in major cities, at airports and bus and train stations.

Photography

I'd like…camera.	**Je voudrais un appareil photo…**
	zhuh voo•dray zuhN nah•pah•rehy foh•toh…
an automatic	**automatique** *oh•toh•mah•teek*
a digital	**numérique** *new•may•reek*
a disposable	**jetable** *zheh•tah•bluh*
I'd like…	**Je voudrais…** *zhuh voo•dray…*
a battery	**une pile** *ewn peel*
digital prints	**des photos numériques**
	day foh•toh new•may•reek
a memory card	**une carte mémoire**
	ewn kahrt may•mwahr
Can I print digital photos here?	**Puis-je imprimer des photos numériques ici ?**
	pwee•zhuh ehN•pree•may day foh•toh
	new•may•reek ee•see

Souvenirs

a bottle of wine	**une bouteille de vin** *ewn boo•tehy duh vehN*
a box of chocolates	**une boîte de chocolats** *ewn bwaht duh shoh•koh•lah*
some crystal	**du cristal** *dew kree•stahl*
a doll	**une poupée** *ewn poo•pay*
some jewelry	**des bijoux** *day bee•zhoo*
a key ring	**un porte-clés** *uhN pohrt•klay*
a postcard	**une carte postale** *ewn kahrt pohs•tahl*
some pottery	**des poteries** *day poh•tuh•ree*
a T-shirt	**un t-shirt** *uhN tee•shuhrt*
a toy	**un jouet** *uhN zhooway*
Can I see this/that ?	**Puis-je voir ceci/cela ?** *pwee•zhuh vwahr suh•see/suh•lah*
I'd like…	**Je voudrais…** *zhuh voo•dray…*
a battery	**une pile** *ewn peel*
a bracelet	**un bracelet** *uhN brahs•lay*
a brooch	**une broche** *ewn brohsh*
a clock	**une pendule** *ewn pawN•dewl*
earrings	**des boucles d'oreille** *day boo•kluh doh•rehy*

a necklace	**un collier** *uhN koh•leeyay*
a ring	**une bague** *ewn bahg*
a watch	**une montre** *ewn mohN•truh*
I'd like…	**Je voudrais…** *zhuh voo•dray…*
copper	**du cuivre** *dew kwee•vruh*
crystal	**du cristal** *dew krees•tahl*
diamonds	**des diamants** *day deeyah•mawN*
white/yellow gold	**de l'or blanc/jaune** *duh lohr blawN/zhohn*
pearls	**des perles** *day pehrl*
pewter	**de l'étain** *duh lay•tehN*
platinum	**du platine** *dew plah•teen*
sterling silver	**de l'argent fin** *duh lahr•zhawN fehN*
Is this real?	**Est-ce que c'est du vrai ?** *ehs kuh say dew vray*
Can you engrave it?	**Pouvez-vous le graver ?**
	poo•vay•voo luh grah•vay

France offers a wide array of souvenirs for the traveler. Souvenir shops are located throughout larger cities, especially near tourist destinations. Certain regions in France are known for their specialty items that make great souvenirs and gifts: lace from Alençon, crystal from Baccarat, perfume from Grasse, porcelain from Limoges and the latest fashions from Paris. Markets and specialty shops are great places to find these regional specialties.

France is well-known for its classic and cutting-edge jewelry design. Paris and the French Riviera are home to famous jewelry houses such as Boucheron®, Cartier® and VanCleef & Arpels®.

Sport & Leisure

ESSENTIAL

When's the game?	**Quand a lieu le match ?** *kawN tah leeyuh luh mahtch*
Where's…?	**Où est…?** *oo ay…*
the beach	**la plage** *lah plazh*
the park	**le parc** *luh pahrk*
the pool	**la piscine** *lah pee·seen*
Is it safe to swim here?	**Est-ce que c'est sans danger de nager ici ?** *ehs kuh say sawN dawN·zhay duh nah·zhay ee·see*
Can I hire clubs?	**Puis-je louer des clubs ?** *pwee·zhuh looway day kluhb*
How much per hour?	**Combien ça coûte par heure ?** *kohN·beeyehN sah koot pahr uhr*
How far is it to…?	**À quelle distance se trouve…?** *ah kehl dees·tawNs suh troov…*
Show me on the map, please.	**Montrez-moi sur la carte, s'il vous plaît.** *mohN·tray·mwah sewr lah kahrt seel voo play*

Watching Sport

When's…(game/ race/tournament)?	**Quand a lieu (le match/la course/ le tournoi)…?** *kawN tah leeyuh (luh mahtch/lah koors/luh toor·nwah)…*
the baseball	**de baseball** *duh bays·bohl*
the basketball	**de basketball** *duh bahs·keht·bohl*
the boxing	**de boxe** *duh bohks*
the cricket	**de cricket** *duh kree·keh*
the cycling	**de cycliste** *duh see·kleest*
the golf	**de golf** *duh gohlf*

the soccer [football]	**de football**	*duh foot·bohl*
the tennis	**de tennis**	*duh tay·nees*
the volleyball	**de volley-ball**	*duh voh·lee·bohl*

Who's playing? **Qui joue ?** *kee zhoo*

Where's the **Où est la piste/le stade ?**
racetrack/stadium ? *oo ay lah peest/luh stahd*

Where can I place a bet? **Où puis-je parier ?** *oo pwee·zhuh pah·reeyay*

For Tickets, see page 18.

Soccer is France's most popular sport. Water sports, such as canoeing, rafting, fishing and sailing, are also popular, not only on the coast, but along scenic lakes and rivers. France is home to the highest peaks in Europe across three mountain ranges: the Alps, the Pyrenees and the Massif Central. Skiing, snowboarding, snowshoeing, hiking and dog sledding are enjoyed there. Other popular sports include cycling, horseback riding, horse racing, golf, paragliding, parachuting and car racing. France is host to many world-renowned sporting events: **Tour de France** bicycle race, **Le Mans** car race and the International Tennis Championships, to name a few.

Casinos can be found in France, especially along the French Riviera. Sports betting is permitted only on horse races.

Playing Sport

Where is/are…?	**Où est/sont…?** *oo ay/sohN…*
the golf course	**le terrain de golf** *luh teh•rehN duh gohlf*
the gym	**le gymnase** *luh zheem•nahz*
the park	**le parc** *luh pahrk*
the tennis courts	**les courts de tennis** *lay koor duh tay•nees*
How much per…	**Combien ça coûte par…?**
	kohN•beeyehN sah koot pahr…
day	**jour** *zhoor*
hour	**heure** *uhr*
game	**partie** *pahr•tee*
round	**tour** *toor*
Can I rent [hire]…?	**Puis-je louer…?** *pwee•zhuh looway…*
some clubs	**des clubs** *day kluhb*
some equipment	**des équipements** *day zay•keep•mawN*
a racket	**une raquette** *ewn rah•keht*

At the Beach/Pool

Where's the beach/pool?	**Où est la plage/piscine?** *oo ay lah plahzh/pee•seen*
Is there a…?	**Y-a-t-il…?** *yah•teel…*
kiddie pool	**une pataugeoire** *ewn pah•toh•zhwahr*
indoor/outdoor pool	**une piscine intérieure/extérieure** *ewn pee•seen ehN•tay•reeyuhr/ehks•tay•reeyuhr*
lifeguard	**un secouriste** *uhN suh•koo•reest*
Is it safe…?	**Est-ce sans danger…?** *ehs sawN dawN•zhay…*
to swim	**de nager** *duh nah•zhay*
to dive	**de plonger** *duh plohN•zhay*
for children	**pour les enfants** *poor lay zawN•fawN*

I'd like to hire…	**Je voudrais louer…** *zhuh voo·dray looway…*
a deck chair	**une chaise** *ewn shehz*
diving equipment	**un équipement de plongée**
	uhN nay·keep·mawN duh plohN·zhay
a jet ski	**un jet ski** *uhN zheht skee*
a motorboat	**un bateau à moteur**
	uhN bah·toh ah moh·tuhr
a rowboat	**une barque** *ewn bahrk*
snorkeling	**un équipement de plongée**
equipment	*uhN ay·keep·mawN duh plohN·zhay*
a surfboard	**un surf** *uhN suhrf*
a towel	**une serviette** *ewn sehr·veeyeht*
an umbrella	**un parasol** *uhN pah·rah·sohl*
water skis	**des skis nautiques** *day skee noh·teek*
a windsurfer	**une planche à voile** *ewn plawNsh ah vwahl*
For…hours.	**Pour…heures.** *poor…uhr*

France has many beaches; the country has long coasts on the English Channel, the Atlantic Ocean and the Mediterranean Sea. Some of the most popular resorts include St. Tropez, Monte Carlo, Cannes, Marseilles, Nice and the island of Corsica in the Mediterranean.

Most beaches have lifeguards on duty during the summer but always check the flags for swimming conditions. A green flag indicates that swimming is allowed, an orange flag indicates swimming is allowed but hazardous, a red flag indicates swimming is not allowed and a yellow flag indicates swimming is inadvisable because of pollution.

Winter Sports

A lift pass for a day/five days, please.	**Un forfait d' un jour/de cinq jours, s'il vous plaît.** *uhN fohr·fay duhN zhoor/duh sehNk zhoor seel voo play*
I'd like to hire...	**Je voudrais louer...** *zhuh voo·dray looway...*
boots	**des bottes** *day boht*
a helmet	**un casque** *uhN kahsk*
poles	**des bâtons** *day bah·tohN*
skis	**des skis** *day skee*
a snowboard	**un snowboard** *uhN snoh·bohrd*
snowshoes	**des raquettes** *day rah·keht*
These are too big/small.	**Ceux-ci m /Celles-ci f /sont trop grands m / grandes f /petits m /petites f /.** *suh·see/sehl·see sohN troh grawN /grawNd/ puh·tee/puh·teet*
Are there lessons?	**Y-a-t-il des leçons ?** *yah·teel day luh·sohN*
I'm a beginner.	**Je suis debutant m /debutante f .** *zhuh swee day·bew·tawN/day·bew·tawNt*
I'm experienced.	**J'ai de l'expérience.** *zhay duh lehk·spay·reeyawNs*
A trail map, please.	**La carte des pistes, s'il vous plaît.** *lah kahrt day peest seel voo play*

YOU MAY SEE…

REMONTÉES	lifts
REMONTE-PENTES	drag lift
TÉLÉPHÉRIQUE	cable car
TÉLÉSIÈGE	chair lift
DÉBUTANT	novice
INTERMÉDIAIRE	intermediate
EXPERT	expert
PISTE FERMÉE	trail [piste] closed

Out in the Country

A map of…, please.	**Une carte…, s'il vous plaît.**
	ewn kahrt…seel voo play
this region	**de cette région** *duh seht ray·zheeyohN*
the walking routes	**des chemins de randonnées**
	day sheh·mehN duh rawN·doh·nay
the bike routes	**des pistes cyclables** *day peest see·klah·bluh*
the trails	**des sentiers** *day sawN·teeyay*
Is it…?	**Est-ce…?** *ehs…*
easy	**facile** *fah·seel*

difficult	**difficile** *dee·fee·seel*
far	**loin** *lwehN*
steep	**escarpé** *ehs·kahr·pay*
How far is it to…?	**À quelle distance se trouve…?**
	ah kehl dees·tawNs suh troov…
I'm lost.	**Je suis perdu** *m* **/perdue** *f.* *zhuh swee pehr·dew*
Where's…?	**Où est…?** *oo ay…*
the bridge	**le pont** *luh pohN*
the cave	**la grotte** *lah groht*
the desert	**le désert** *luh day·zehr*
the farm	**la ferme** *lah fehrm*
the field	**le champ** *luh shawN*
the forest	**la forêt** *lah foh·reh*
the hill	**la colline** *lah koh·leen*
the lake	**le lac** *luh lahk*
the mountain	**la montagne** *lah mohN·tah·nyuh*
the nature preserve	**le parc naturel** *luh pahrk nah·tew·rehl*
the viewpoint	**le point d'observation**
	luh pwehNdohb·sehr·vah·seeyohN
the park	**le parc** *luh pahrk*
the path	**le chemin** *luh shuh·mehN*
the peak	**le sommet** *luh soh·may*
the picnic area	**l'aire de pique-nique** *lehr duh peek·neek*
the pond	**l'étang** *lay·tawN*
the river	**la rivière** *lah ree·veeyehr*
the sea	**la mer** *lah mehr*
the (hot) spring	**la source (d'eau chaude)** *lah soors (doh shohd)*
the stream	**le ruisseau** *luh rwee·soh*
the valley	**la vallée** *lah vah·lay*
the vineyard	**la vigne** *lah vee·nyuh*
the waterfall	**les cascades** *lay kahs·kahd*

Going Out

ESSENTIAL

What's there to do at night?	**Que peut-on faire le soir ?** *kuh puh•tohN fehr luh swahr*
Do you have a program of events?	**Avez-vous un programme des festivités ?** *ah•vay•voo uhN proh•grahm day fehs•tee•vee•tay*
What's playing tonight?	**Qui joue ce soir ?** *kee zhoo suh swahr*
Where's...?	**Où est...?** *oo ay...*
the downtown area	**le centre ville** *luh sawN•truh veel*
the bar	**le bar** *luh bahr*
the dance club	**la discothèque** *lah dees•koh•tehk*

Entertainment

Can you recommend...?	**Pouvez-vous me conseiller...?** *poo•vay•voo muh kohN•say•yay...*
a concert	**un concert** *uhN kohN•sehr*
a movie	**un film** *uhN feelm*
an opera	**un opéra** *uhN noh•pay•rah*

a play	**une pièce de théâtre** *ewn peeyehs duh tay•ah•truh*
When does it start/end ?	**Quand est-ce que ça commence/finit ?** *kawN tehs kuh sah koh•mawNs/fee•nee*
What's the dress code?	**Quelle est la tenue exigée ?** *kehl ay lah tuh•new ehk•see•zhay*
I like…	**J'aime…** *zhehm…*
classical music	**la musique classique** *lah mew•zeek klah•seek*
folk music	**la musique folklorique** *lah mew•zeek fohl•kloh•reek*
jazz	**le jazz** *luh zhahz*
pop music	**la pop musique** *lah pohp mew•zeek*
rap	**le rap** *luh rahp*

For Tickets, see page 18.

Tourist information offices can provide information on local entertainment. Newspapers will usually list upcoming events. In the larger cities, there are magazines and publications that list the bars, clubs and other venues and activities of interest. These magazines can usually be found in bookstores or newsstands. Your hotel concierge can also help you find entertainment options.

You May Hear…

Éteignez vos portables, s'il vous plaît.   Turn off your mobile
ay·teh·nyay voh pohr·tah·bluh seel voo play   phones, please.

Nightlife

What's there to do at night?	**Que peut-on faire le soir ?** *kuh puh·tohN fehr luh swahr*
Can you recommend…?	**Pouvez-vous me conseiller…?** *poo·vay·voo muh kohN·say·yay…*
a bar	**un bar** *uhN bahr*
a cabaret	**un cabaret** *uhN kah·bah·ray*
a casino	**un casino** *uhN kah·zee·noh*
a dance club	**une discothèque** *ewn dees·koh·tehk*
a gay club	**un club gay** *uhN kluhb gay*
a jazz club	**un club de jazz** *uhN kluhb duh zhahz*
a club with French music	**un club de musique française** *uhN kluhb duh mew·zeek frawN·sehz*
Is there live music?	**Y-a-t-il des concerts?** *yah·teel day kohN·sehr*
How do I get there?	**Comment est-ce que je m'y rends ?** *koh·mawN tehs kuh zhuh mee rawN*
Is there a cover charge?	**Y-a-t-il un droit d'entrée ?** *yah·teel uhN drwah dawN·tray*
Let's go dancing.	**Allons danser.** *ah·lohN dawN·say*
Is this area safe at night?	**Est-ce que cet endroit est sûr la nuit ?** *ehs kuh seht awN·drwah ay sewr lah nwee*

Special Requirements

Business Travel   145
Traveling with Children 148
Disabled Travelers   152

Business Travel

ESSENTIAL

I'm here on business.	**Je suis ici pour affaires.** *zhuh swee zee•see poo rah•fehr*
Here's my card.	**Voici ma carte.** *vwah•see mah kahrt*
Can I have your card?	**Puis-je avoir votre carte ?** *pwee•zhuh ah•vwahr voh•truh kahrt*
I have a meeting with...	**J'ai une réunion avec...** *zhay ewn ray•ew•neeyohN nah•vehk...*
Where's...?	**Où est...?** *oo ay...*
the business center	**le centre d'affaires** *luh sawN•truh dah•fehr*
the convention hall	**le palais des congrès** *luh pah•lay day kohN•greh*
the meeting room	**la salle de réunion** *lah sahl duh ray•ew•neeyohN*

The customary greeting for business people is a firm handshake.
Last names are used instead of first names when meeting someone;
say, **Bonjour, monsieur/madame Ferrard** for example. It is polite to
be on time for business meetings.

On Business

I'm here for...	**Je suis ici pour...** *zhuh swee zee•see poor...*
a seminar	**un séminaire** *uhN say•mee•nehr*
a conference	**une conférence** *ewn kohN•fay•rawNs*
a meeting	**une réunion** *ewn ray•ew•neeyohN*
My name is...	**Je m'appelle...** *zhuh mah•pehl...*
May I introduce my colleague...	**Puis-je vous présenter mon *m*/ma *f* collègue...** *pwee•zhuh voo pray•zawN•tay mohN /mah koh•lehg...*

Pleasure to meet you.	**J'ai été ravi** *m* **/ravie** *f* **de faire votre connaissance.** *zhay ay•tay rah•vee duh fehr voh•truh koh•neh•sawNs*
I have a meeting/an appointment with…	**J'ai une réunion/un rendez-vous avec…** *zhay ewn ray•ew•neeyohN/uhN rawN•day•voo ah•vehk…*
I'm sorry I'm late.	**Je suis désolé** *m* **/désolée** *f* **je suis en retard.** *zhuh swee day•zoh•lay zhuh swee zawN ruh•tahr*
I need an interpreter.	**J'ai besoin d'un interprète.** *zhay buh•zwehN duhN nehN•tehr•preht*
You can contact me at the…Hotel.	**Vous pouvez me joindre à l'hôtel…** *voo poo•vay muh zhwehN•druh ah loh•tehl…*
I'm here until…	**Je suis ici jusqu'à…** *zhuh swee zee•see zhew•skah…*
I need to…	**J'ai besoin…** *zhay buh•zwehN…*
make a call	**de téléphoner** *duh tay•lay•foh•nay*
make a photocopy	**de faire une photocopie** *duh fehr ewn foh•toh•koh•pee*
send an e-mail	**d'envoyer un mail** *dawN•vwah•yay uhN mehl*
send a fax	**d'envoyer un fax** *dawN•vwah•yay uhN fahks*

| send a package (for next-day delivery) | **d'envoyer un colis** *(avec livraison le jour suivant) dawN·vwah·yay uhN koh·lee (ah·vehk lee·vray·zohN luh zhoor swee·vawN)* |
| It was a pleasure to meet you. | **J'ai été ravi** *m* **/ravie** *f* **de faire votre connaissance.** *zhay ay·tay rah·vee duh fehr voh·truh koh·neh·sawNs* |

For Communications, see page 48.

YOU MAY HEAR...

Avez-vous un rendez-vous ? *ah·vay·voo zuhN rawN·day·voo*	Do you have an appointment?
Avec qui ? *ah·vehk kee*	With whom?
Il *m* **/Elle** *f* **est en réunion.** *Eel/ehl ay tawN ray·ew·neeyohN*	He/She is in a meeting.
Un instant, s'il vous plaît. *uhN nehN·stawN seel voo play*	One moment, please.
Asseyez-vous. *ah·seh·yay·voo*	Have a seat.
Voulez-vous boire quelque chose ? *voo·lay·voo bwahr kehl·kuh shohz*	Would you like something to drink?
Merci de votre visite. *mehr·see duh voh·truh vee·zeet*	Thank you for coming.

Traveling with Children

Essential

Is there a discount for kids?	**Y-a-t-il une remise pour les enfants ?** *yah·teel ewn ruh·meez poor lay zawN·fawN*
Can you recommend a babysitter?	**Pouvez-vous me recommander une baby-sitter ?** *poo·vay·voo muh ruh·koh·mawN·day ewn bah·bee·see·tuhr*
Do you have a child's seat/highchair?	**Avez-vous un siège enfant/une chaise haute ?** *ah·vay·voo zuhN seeyehzh awN·fawN/ zewn shehz oht*
Where can I change the baby?	**Où puis-je changer le bébé ?** *oo pwee·zhuh shawN·zhay luh bay·bay*

Out & About

Can you recommend something for kids?	**Pouvez-vous me conseiller quelque chose pour les enfants ?** *poo·vay·voo muh kohN·say·yay kehl·kuh shohz poor lay zawN·fawN*
Where's…?	**Où est…?** *oo ay…*
the amusement park	**le parc d'attractions** *luh pahrk dah·trahk·seeyohN*
the arcade	**la salle de jeux** *lah sahl duh zhuh*
the kiddie [paddling] pool	**la pataugeoire** *lah pah·toh·zhwahr*
the park	**le parc** *luh pahrk*
the playground	**l'aire de jeux** *lehr duh zhuh*
the zoo	**le zoo** *luh zoh*
Are kids allowed?	**Est-ce que les enfants sont autorisés ?** *ehs kuh lay zawN·fawN sohN toh·toh·ree·zay*

| Is it safe for kids? | **Est-ce que c'est sans danger pour les enfants ?** *ehs kuh say sawN dawN•zay poor lay zawN•fawN* |
| Is it suitable for…year olds? | **Est-ce que cela convient aux enfants de…ans ?** *ehs kuh suh•lah kohN•veeyehN oh zawN•fawN duh…awN* |

For Numbers, see page 173.

YOU MAY HEAR…

Comme il _m_ /elle _f_ est mignon _m_ / mignonne _f_ ! *kohm eel/ehl aymee•nyohN/mee•nyohn*	How cute!
Comment s'appelle-t-il _m_ /elle _f_ ? *koh•mawN sah•pehl•teel/tehl*	What's his/her name?
Quel âge a-t-il _m_ /a-t-elle _f_ ? *kehl ahzh ah•teel/ah•tehl*	How old is he/she?

Baby Essentials

| Do you have…? | **Avez-vous…?** *ah•vay•voo…* |
| a baby bottle | **un biberon** *uhN bee•buh•rohN* |

baby food	**des petits pots** *day puh•tee poh*
baby wipes	**des lingettes pour bébé** *day lehN•zhet poor bay•bay*
a car seat	**un siège bébé** *uhN seeyehzh bay•bay*
a children's menu/portion	**un menu/des portions pour enfants** *uhN muh•new/day pohr•seeyohN poo rawN•fawN*
a child's seat/ highchair	**un siège bébé/une chaise haute** *uhN seeyehzh bay•bay/ewn shehz oht*
a crib/cot	**un berceau/lit pliant** *uhN behr•soh/ lee pleeyawN*
diapers [nappies]	**des couches** *day koosh*
formula	**du lait pour bébé** *dew lay poor bay•bay*
a pacifier [dummy]	**une tétine** *ewn tay•teen*
a playpen	**un parc pour enfant** *uhN pahrk poo rawN•fawN*
a stroller [pushchair]	**une poussette** *ewn poo•seht*
Can I breastfeed the baby here?	**Puis-je allaiter le bébé ici ?** *pwee•zhuh ah•leh•tay luh bay•bay ee•see*

Where can I breastfeed/change the baby?	**Où puis-je allaiter/changer le bébé ?** *oo pwee•zhuh ah•leh•tay/shawN•zhay luh bay•bay*

For Dining with Children, see page 65.
For Meals & Cooking, see page 67.

Babysitting

Can you recommend a babysitter?	**Pouvez-vous me recommander une baby-sitter ?** *poo•vay•voo muh ruh•koh•mawN•day ewn bah•bee•see•tuhr*
How much do you/they charge?	**Quel est votre/leur tarif ?** *kehl ay voh•truh/luhr tah•reef*
I'll be back at…	**Je reviens à…** *zhuh ruh•veeyehN ah…*
If you need to contact me, call…	**Si vous avez besoin de me contacter, appelez…** *see voo sah•vay buh•swehN duh muh kohN•tahk•tay ah•play…*

Health & Emergency

Can you recommend a pediatrician?	**Pouvez-vous me recommander un pédiatre ?** *poo•vay•voo muh ruh•koh•mawN•day uhN pay•deeyah•truh*
My child is allergic to…	**Mon enfant est allergique à…** *mohN nawN•fawN ay ah•lehr•zheek ah…*
My child is missing.	**Mon enfant a disparu.** *mohN nawN•fawN ah dees•pah•rew*
Have you seen a boy/girl?	**Avez-vous vu un garçon/une fille ?** *ah•vay•voo vew uhN gahr•sohN/ewn fee•yuh*

For Police, see page 156.
For Health, see page 158.

Disabled Travelers

ESSENTIAL

Is there...?	**Y-a-t-il...?** *yah·teel...*
access for	**un accès pour handicapés**
the disabled	*uhN nahk·seh poor awN·dee·kah·pay*
a wheelchair ramp	**un accès pour chaises roulantes**
	uhN nahk·say poor shehz roo·lawNt
a disabled-	**des toilettes accessibles aux handicapés**
toilet	*day twah·leht ahk·seh·see·bluh*
accessible toilet	*oh zawN·dee·kah·pay*
I need...	**J'ai besoin...** *zhay buh·zwehN...*
assistance	**d'aide** *dehd*
an elevator [a lift]	**d'un ascenseur** *duhN nah·sawN·suhr*
a ground-floor	**d'une chambre au rez-de-chaussée**
room	*dewn shawN·bruh oh ray·duh·shoh·say*

Asking for Assistance

I'm...	**Je suis...** *zhuh swee...*
disabled	**handicapé** *m* /**handicapée** *f*
	awN·dee·kah·pay
visually impaired	**malvoyant** *m* /**malvoyante** *f*
	mahl·vwah·yawN/mahl·vwah·yawNt
deaf	**sourd** *m* /**sourde** *f* *soor/soord*
hearing impaired	**malentendant** *m* /**malentendante** *f*
	mah·lawN·tawN·dawN/ mah·lawN·tawN·dahNt

unable to walk far/use the stairs	**incapable de marcher longtemps/ d'utiliser les escaliers** *ehN·kah·pah·bluh duh mahr·shay lohN·tawN/ dew·tee·lee·zay lay zehs·kah·leeyay*
Please speak louder.	**S'il vous plaît, parlez plus fort.** *seel voo play pahr·lay plew fohr*
Can I bring my wheelchair?	**Puis-je apporter ma chaise roulante ?** *pwee·zhuh ah·pohr·tay mah shehz roo·lawNt*
Are guide dogs permitted?	**Est-ce que les chiens de guide sont autorisés ?** *ehs kuh lay sheeyehN duh geed sohN toh·toh·ree·zay*
Can you help me?	**Pouvez-vous m'aider ?** *poo·vay·voo mehy·day*
Please open/hold the door.	**S'il vous plaît, ouvrez/tenez la porte.** *seel voo play oo·vray/tuh·nay lah pohrt*

In an Emergency

Emergencies	155
Police	156
Health	158
The Basics	167

Emergencies

ESSENTIAL

Help!	**Au secours !** *oh suh•koor*
Go away!	**Allez-vous en !** *ah•lay•voo zawN*
Stop, thief!	**Arrêtez, au voleur !** *ah•reh•tay oh voh•luhr*
Get a doctor!	**Allez chercher un docteur !** *ah•lay shehr•shay uhN dohk•tuhr*
Fire!	**Au feu !** *oh fuh*
I'm lost.	**Je suis perdu m /perdue f.** *zhuh swee pehr•dew*
Can you help me?	**Pouvez-vous m'aider ?** *poo•vay•voo may•day*

In an emergency, dial: **17** for the police
18 for the fire brigade
15 for the ambulance

YOU MAY HEAR...

Remplissez ce formulaire. *rawN•plee•say suh fohr•mew•lehr*	Fill out this form.
Vos papiers d'identité, s'il vous plaît. *voh pah•peeyay dee•dawN•tee•tay seel voo play*	Your ID, please.
Quand/Où cela s'est-il produit ? *kawN/oo suh•lah say•teel proh•dwee*	When/Where did it happen?
À quoi ressemble-t-il m / ressemble-t-elle f? *ah kwah ruh•sawN•bluh•teel/ruh•sawN•bluh•tehl*	What does he/she look like?

Police

ESSENTIAL

Call the police!	**Appelez la police !** *ah·puh·lay lah poh·lees*
Where's the police station?	**Où est le commissariat de police ?** *oo ay luh koh·mee·sah·reeyah duh poh·lees*
There was an accident/attack.	**Il y a eu un accident/une attaque.** *eel·yah ew uhN nahk·see·dawN/ewn ah·tahk*
My child is missing.	**Mon enfant a disparu.** *mohN nawN·fawN ah dees·pah·rew*
I need an interpreter/to make a phone call.	**J'ai besoin d'un interprète/de téléphoner.** *zhay buh·zwehN duhN nehN·tehr·preht/ duh tay·lay·foh·nay*
I'm innocent.	**Je suis innocent m /innocente f.** *zhuh swee zee·noh·sawN/zee·noh·sawNt*

Crime & Lost Property

I want to report...	**Je voudrais signaler...** *zhuh voo·dray see·nyah·lay...*
a mugging	**une attaque** *ewn ah·tahk*
a rape	**un viol** *uhN veeyohl*
a theft	**un vol** *uhN vohl*
I've been mugged.	**J'ai été attaqué m /attaquée f.** *zhay ay·tay ah·tah·kay*
I've been robbed.	**J'ai été dévalisé m /dévalisée f.** *zhay ay·tay day·vah·lee·zay*
I've lost...	**J'ai perdu...** *zhay pehr·dew...*
...was stolen.	**...a été vole m /volée f. ...** *ah ay·tay voh·lay*
My backpack	**Mon sac-à-dos** *mohN sahk·ah·doh*

My bicycle	**Mon vélo** *mohN vay•loh*
My camera	**Mon appareil photo** *mohN nah•pah•rehy foh•toh*
My (hire) car	**Ma voiture (de location)** *mah vwah•tuhr (duh loh•kah•seeyohN)*
My computer	**Mon ordinateur** *mohN nohr•dee•nah•tuhr*
My credit card	**Ma carte de crédit** *mah kahrt duh kray•dee*
My jewelry	**Mes bijoux** *may bee•zhoo*
My money	**Mon argent** *mohN nahr•zhawN*
My passport	**Mon passeport** *mohN pahs•pohr*
My purse [handbag]	**Mon sac** *mohN sahk*
My traveller's cheques	**Mes chèques de voyage** *may shehk duh vwah•yahzh*
My wallet	**Mon porte-feuille** *mohN pohrt•fuhy*
I need a police report.	**J'ai besoin d'un constat de police.** *zhay buh•zwehN duhN kohN•stah duh poh•lees*
Where is the British/ American/Irish embassy?	**Où est l'ambassade britannique/ américaine/irlandaise ?** *oo ay lawN•bah•sahd bree•tah•neek/ah•may•ree•kayn/eer•lawN•dayz*

Health

ESSENTIAL

I'm sick .	**Je suis malade.** *zhuh swee mah·lahd*
I need an English-speaking doctor.	**J'ai besoin d'un docteur qui parle anglais.** *zhay buh·zwehN duhN dohk·tuhr kee pahrl awN·glay*
It hurts here.	**Ça fait mal ici.** *sah fay mahl ee·see*

Finding a Doctor

Can you recommend a doctor/dentist?	**Pouvez-vous me recommander un docteur/dentiste ?** *poo·vay·voo muh ruh·koh·mawN·day uhN dohk·tuhr/dawN·teest*
Can the doctor come here?	**Est-ce que le docteur peut venir ici ?** *ehs kuh luh dohk·tuhr puh veh·neer ee·see*
I need an English-speaking doctor.	**J'ai besoin d'un docteur qui parle anglais.** *zhay buh·zwehN duhN dohk·tuhr kee pahrl awN·glay*
What are the office hours?	**Quelles sont les heures d'ouverture ?** *kehl sohN lay zuhr doo·vehr·tewr*
I'd like an appointment for...	**Je voudrais un rendez-vous pour...** *zhuh voo·dray uhN rawN·day-voo poor...*
today	**aujourd'hui** *oh·zhoor·dwee*
tomorrow	**demain** *duh·mehN*
as soon as possible	**le plus vite possible** *luh plew veet poh·see·bluh*
It's urgent.	**C'est urgent.** *say tewr·zhawN*

Symptoms

I'm bleeding.	**Je saigne.** *zhuh sehnyuh*
I'm constipated.	**Je suis constipé m /constipée f.** *zhuh swee kohN·stee·pay*

I'm dizzy.	**J'ai des vertiges.** *zhay day vehr•teezh*
I'm nauseous.	**J'ai des nausées.** *zhay day noh•zay*
I'm vomiting.	**Je vomis.** *zhuh voh•mee*
It hurts here.	**J'ai mal ici.** *zhay mahl ee•see*
I have…	**J'ai…** *zhay…*
an allergic reaction	**une réaction allergique** *ewn reh•ahk•seeyohN ah•lehr•zheek*
chest pain	**une douleur à la poitrine** *ewn doo•luhr ah lah pwah•treen*
cramps	**des crampes** *day krawNp*
diarrhea	**la diarrhée** *lah deeyah•ray*
an earache	**mal aux oreilles** *mahl oh zoh•rehy*
a fever	**de la fièvre** *duh lah feeyeh•vruh*
pain	**mal** *mahl*
a rash	**une irritation cutanée** *ewn ee•ree•tah•seeyohN kew•tah•nay*
a sprain	**une entorse** *ewn awN•tohrs*
some swelling	**une grosseur** *ewn groh•suhr*
a sore throat	**un mal de gorge** *uhN mahl duh gohrzh*
a stomachache	**mal au ventre** *mahl oh vawN•truh*
I've been sick for…days.	**Je suis malade depuis…jours.** *zhuh swee mah•lahd duh•pwee…zhoor*

For Numbers, see page 173.

Conditions

I'm…	**Je suis…** *zhuh swee…*
anemic	**anémique** *ah•nay•meek*
asthmatic	**asthmatique** *ahs•mah•teek*
diabetic	**diabétique** *deeyah•bay•teek*
epileptic	**épileptique** *ay•peel•ay•pteek*

159

I'm allergic to antibiotics/penicillin.	**Je suis allergique aux antibiotiques/à la pénicilline.** *zhuh swee zah·lehr·zheek oh zawN·tee·beeyoh·teek/ah lah pay·nee·see·leen*
I have…	**J'ai…** *zhay…*
arthritis	**de l'arthrite** *duh lahr·treet*
a heart condition	**un problème cardiaque** *uhN proh·blehm kahr·deeyahk*
high/low blood pressure	**une tension élevée/basse** *ewn tawN·seeyohN ay·luh·vay/bahs*
I'm on…	**Je prends…** *zhuh prawN…*

YOU MAY HEAR…

Qu'est-ce qui ne va pas ? *kehs kee nuh vah pah*	What's wrong?
Où est-ce que ça fait mal ? *oo ehs kuh sah fay mahl*	Where does it hurt?
Est-ce que ça fait mal ici ? *ehs kuh sah fay mahl ee·see*	Does it hurt here?
Prenez-vous des médicaments ? *prueh·nay·voo day may·dee·kah·mawN*	Are you on medication?

Êtes-vous allergique à quelque chose ? *eht·voo zah·lehr·zheek ah kehl·kuh shohz* — Are you allergic to anything?

Ouvrez la bouche. *oo·vray lah boosh* — Open your mouth.

Respirez profondément. *rehs·pee·ray proh·fohN·day·mawN* — Breathe deeply.

Toussez, s'il vous plaît. *too·say seel voo play* — Cough, please.

Allez à l'hôpital. *ah·lay ah loh·pee·tahl* — Go to the hospital.

Treatment

Do I need a prescription/medicine?	**Ai-je besoin d'une ordonnance/de médicaments ?** *ay·zhuh buh·zwehN dewn ohr·doh·nawNs/duh meh·dee·kah·mawN*
Can you prescribe a generic drug [unbranded medication]?	**Pouvez-vous me prescrire un médicament générique ?** *poo·vay·voo muh prehs·kreer uhN may·dee·kah·mawN zhay·nay·reek*
Where can I get it?	**Où puis-je l'obtenir ?** *oo pwee·zhuh lohb·tuh·neer*

For Pharmacy, see page 163.

Hospital

Notify my family, please.	**Informez ma famille, s'il vous plaît.** *ehN·fohr·may mah fah·meeyuh seel voo play*
I'm in pain.	**J'ai mal.** *zhay mahl*
I need a doctor/nurse.	**J'ai besoin d'un docteur/d'une infirmière.** *zhay buh·zwehN duhN dohk·tuhr/dewn ehN·feer·meeyehr*
When are visiting hours?	**Quand sont les heures de visite ?** *kawN sohN lay zuhr duh vee·zeet*
I'm visiting...	**Je viens voir...** *zhuh veeyehN vwahr...*

Dentist

I have…	**J'ai…** *zhay…*
a broken tooth	**une dent cassée** *ewn dawN kah•say*
a lost filling	**perdu un plombage** *pehr•dew uhN plohN•bahzh*
a toothache	**mal aux dents** *mahl oh dawN*
Can you fix this denture?	**Pouvez-vous réparer ce dentier ?** *poo•vay•voo ray•pah•ray suh dawN•teeyay*

Gynecologist

I have cramps/ a vaginal infection.	**J'ai des crampes/une infection vaginale.** *zhay day krawNp/ewn ehN•fehk•seeyohN vah•zhee•nahl*
I missed my period.	**Je n'ai pas eu mes règles.** *zhuh nay pah ew may reh•gluh*
I'm on the Pill.	**Je prends la pillule.** *zhuh prawN lah pee•lewl*
I'm (…months) pregnant.	**Je suis enceinte (de…mois).** *zhuh swee zawN•sehNt (duh…mwah)*
I'm not pregnant.	**Je ne suis pas enceinte.** *zhuh nuh swee pah zawN•sehNt*
My last period was…	**Mes dernières règles étaient…** *may dehr•neeyehr reh•gluh ay•tay…*

For Numbers, see page 173.

Optician

I've lost…	**J'ai perdu…** *zhay pehr•dew…*
a contact lens	**une lentille de contact** *ewn lawN•tee•yuh duh kohN•tahk*
my glasses	**mes lunettes** *may lew•neht*
a lens	**une lentille** *ewn lawN•tee•yuh*

Payment & Insurance

How much?	**Combien ça coûte ?** *kohN•beeyehN sah koot*
Can I pay by credit card?	**Puis-je payer par carte ?** *pwee•zhuh pay•yay pahr kahrt*
I have insurance.	**J'ai une assurance.** *zhay ewn ah•sew•rawNs*
I need a receipt for my insurance.	**J'ai besoin d'un reçu pour ma compagnie d'assurance.** *zhay buh•zwehN duhN ruh•sew poor mah kohN•pah•nee dah•sew•rawNs*

Pharmacy

ESSENTIAL

Where's the pharmacy?	**Où est la pharmacie ?** *oo ay lah fahr•mah•see*
What time does it open/close?	**À quelle heure ouvre-t-elle/ferme-t-elle ?** *ah kehl uhr oo•vruh•tehl/fehrm•tehl*
What would you recommend for...?	**Que me conseillez-vous pour...?** *kuh muh kohN•say•yay•voo poor...*
How much do I take?	**Combien dois-je en prendre ?** *kohN•beeyehN dwah•zhuh awN prawN•druh*
I'm allergic to...	**Je suis allergique à...** *zhuh swee zah•lehr•zheek ah...*

Pharmacies can be identified by the green cross-shaped neon light on display. Pharmacies are usually open from 9:00 a.m. to 6:00 p.m. without closing for lunch. Some pharmacies are open from 8:00 a.m. to 2:00 a.m. or even 24 hours, especially in the larger cities; a list of 24-hour pharmacies can be found on the door of every pharmacy. Some doctors still make house calls; ask your concierge for more information.

What to Take

How much do I take?	**Combien dois-je en prendre ?** *kohN•beeyehN dwah•zhuh awN prawN•druh*
How often?	**Combien de fois ?** *kohN•beeyehN duh fwah*
Is it safe for children?	**Est-ce sans danger pour les enfants ?** *ehs sawN dawN•zay poor lay zawN•fawN*
I'm taking…	**Je prends…** *zhuh prawN…*
Are there side effects?	**Y-a-t-il des effets secondaires ?** *yah•teel day zeh•feh suh•kohN•dehr*
I need something for…	**J'ai besoin de quelque chose pour soigner…** *zhay buh•zwehN duh kehl•kuh shohz poor swah•nyay…*
a cold	**un rhume** *uhN rewm*
a cough	**une toux** *ewn too*
diarrhea	**une diarrhée** *ewn deeyah•ray*
a headache	**un mal de tête** *uhN mahl duh tayt*
insect bites	**des piqures d'insectes** *day pee•kewr dehN•sehkt*
motion sickness	**le mal des transports** *luh mahl day trawNs•pohr*
a sore throat	**un mal à la gorge** *uhN mahl ah lah gohrzh*
sunburn	**un coup de soleil** *uhN koo duh soh•lehy*
a toothache	**un mal de dents** *uhN mahl duh dawN*
an upset stomach	**un mal au ventre** *uhN mahl oh vawN•truh*

YOU MAY SEE…

UNE/TROIS FOIS PAR JOUR	once/three times a day
UN CACHET	tablet
UNE GOUTTE	drop
UNE CUILLÈRE	teaspoon

...LES REPAS	...meals
APRÈS	after
AVANT	before
PENDANT	with
À JEUN	on an empty stomach
À AVALER	swallow whole
RISQUE DE SOMNOLENCE	may cause drowsiness
NE PAS AVALER	do not ingest

Basic Supplies

I'd like...	**Je voudrais...** *zhuh voo·dray...*
acetaminophen [paracetamol]	**du paracétamol** *dew pah·rah·say·tah·mohl*
antiseptic cream	**une crème antiseptique** *ewn krehm awN·tee·sehp·teek*
aspirin	**une aspirine** *ewn ahs·pee·reen*
bandages	**des pansements** *day pawNs·mawN*
a comb	**un peigne** *uhN peh·nyuh*
condoms	**des préservatifs** *day pray·sehr·vah·teef*

contact lens solution	**de la solution pour lentilles de contact** *duh lah soh·lew·seeyohN poor lawN·tee·yuh duh kohN·tahk*
deodorant	**du déodorant** *dew day·oh·doh·rawN*
a hairbrush	**une brosse à cheveux** *ewn brohs ah shuh·vuh*
hairspray	**de la laque** *duh lah lahk*
ibuprofen	**de l'ibuprofène** *duh lee·bew·proh·fehn*
insect repellent	**de la lotion anti-insectes** *duh lah loh·seeyohN awN·tee·ehN·sehkt*
lotion	**une lotion** *ewn loh·seeyohN*
a nail file	**une lime à ongle** *ewn leem ah ohN·gluh*
a (disposable) razor	**un rasoir (jetable)** *uhN rah·zwahr (zhuh·tah·bluh)*
razor blades	**des lames de rasoir** *day lahm duh rah·zwahr*
sanitary napkins [towels]	**des serviettes hygiéniques** *day sehr·veeyeht ee·zheeyay·neek*
shampoo/ conditioner	**du shampooing/de l'après shampooing** *dew shawN·poo·wehN/duh lah·preh shawN·poo·wehN*
soap	**du savon** *dew sah·vohN*
sunscreen	**de la crème solaire** *duh lah krehm soh·lehr*
tampons	**des tampons** *day tawN·pohN*
tissues	**des Kleenex®** *day klee·nehks*
toilet paper	**du papier toilette** *dew pah·peeyay twah·leht*
toothpaste	**du dentifrice** *dew dehN·tee·frees*

For Baby Essentials, see page 149.

The Basics

Grammar

Regular Verbs

Regular French verbs follow a set pattern for conjugation. Remove the **-er**, **-ir** or **-re** ending and replace it with the correct ending for the tense and gender. See the tables below for examples of regular **-er**, **-ir** and **-re** verbs and the appropriate endings (in bold).

French uses subject pronouns (I, you, he, etc.) in much the same ways as English does. The first-person singular subject pronoun (I) is **je**. **Je** is abbreviated to **j'** if the following word begins with a vowel.

PARLER (to speak)		Present	Past	Future
I	**je/j'**	par**le**	ai parlé	parler**ai**
you (sing.)	**tu**	par**les**	as parlé	parler**as**
he/she	**il** m /**elle** f	par**le**	a parlé	parler**a**
we	**nous**	par**lons**	avons parlé	parler**ons**
you (pl.)	**vous**	par**l**	avez parlé	parler**ez**
they	**ils** m /**elles** f	par**lent**	ont parlé	parler**ont**

CHOISIR (to choose)		Present	Past	Future
I	**je/j'**	chois**is**	ai choisi	choisir**ai**
you (sing.)	**tu**	chois**is**	as choisi	choisir**as**
he/she	**il** m /**elle** f	chois**it**	a choisi	choisir**a**
we	**nous**	chois**issons**	avons choisi	choisir**ons**
you (pl.)	vous	chois**issez**	avez choisi	choisir**ez**
they	**ils** m /**elles** f	chois**issent**	ont choisi	choisir**ont**

ATTENDRE (to wait for)		Present	Past	Future
I	je/j'	attends	ai attendu	attendrai
you (sing.)	tu	attends	as attendu	attendras
he/she	il *m*/elle *f*	attend	a attendu	attendra
we	nous	attendons	avons attendu	attendrons
you (pl.)	vous	attendez	avez attendu	attendrez
they	ils *m*/elles *f*	attendent	ont attendu	attendrent

Irregular Verbs

There are many irregular verbs that do not follow the standard conjugation rules and must be memorized. Two common irregular verbs are **avoir** (to have) and **être** (to be). **Avoir** and **être** are used as auxiliary verbs in the past tense. Most verbs use **avoir**, but several common, important verbs use **être**. In general, verbs of coming and going use **être** in the past tense, e.g., **aller** (to go), **venir** (to come), **sortir** (to go out), **partir** (to leave) and **arrive** (to arrive).

AVOIR (to have)

I have	j'ai
you (sing.) have	tu as
he/she has	il *m*/elle *f* a
we have	nous avons
you (pl.) have	vous avez
they have	ils *m*/elles *f* ont

ÊTRE (to be)

I am	je suis
you (sing.) are	tu es
he/she is	il *m*/elle *f* est
we are	nous sommes

| you (pl.) are | **vous êtes** |
| they are | **ils** *m* /**elles** *f* **sont** |

Word Order

French sentences are constructed as in English: subject, verb, object.

Example: **Nous achetons un livre.** We're buying a book.

Questions can be formed in four different ways. The easiest is to just raise your voice at the end of a sentence:

Vous parlez anglais ? You speak English?

You can also add **n'est-ce pas** (isn't that so/right) at the end of a phrase:

Vous parlez anglais, n'est-ce pas ? You speak English, right?

You can put est-ce que in front of a phrase:

Est-ce que vous parlez anglais ? Do you speak English?

You can also put the verb before the subject:

Parlez-vous anglais ? Do you speak English?

(literally: Speak you English?)

Negations

Negative sentences are generally formed by adding **ne** before the verb and **pas** after it. When spoken, the **ne** is often dropped.

Example: **Nous fumons.** We smoke.

Nous ne fumons pas. We do not smoke.

Imperatives

Most imperatives are formed by using the stem of the verb with the appropriate ending.

you (sing.)	**tu**	**Parle !**	Speak!	**Attends !**	Wait!
we	**nous**	**Parlons !**	Let's speak!	**Attendons!**	Let's wait!
you (pl.)	**vous**	**Parlez !**	Speak!	**Attendez !**	Wait!

Nouns & Articles

In French, nouns are either masculine or feminine. The singular definite articles (the) are **le**, for masculine nouns, and **la**, for feminine nouns. **Les** is the plural definite article for both masculine and feminine nouns. Generally, nouns ending in **-e**, **-té** and **-tion** are feminine and take **la**.

Gender	Singular		Plural	
masculine	**le train**	the train	**les trains**	the trains
feminine	**la table**	the table	**les tables**	the tables

The singular indefinite articles (a/an) are **un**, for masculine nouns, and **une**, for feminine nouns. **Des** is the plural indefinite article for both masculine and feminine nouns.

Gender	Singular		Plural	
masculine	**un train**	a train	**des trains**	trains
feminine	**une table**	a table	**des tables**	tables

Adjectives

Adjectives describe nouns and must agree with the noun in gender and number. To form the feminine of many common adjectives, add **-e** to the masculine; if the word already ends in **-e** there is no change. To form the plural adjective, add **-s** to the end; if the word already ends in **-s** there is no change.

Examples:

un livre intéressant	an interesting book
des livres intéresssants	interesting books
une fille intéressante	an interesting girl
des filles intéressantes	interesting girls

Comparatives & Superlatives

Comparatives are formed by adding **plus** (more) or **moins** (less) before
the adjective. Superlatives are formed by adding **le** *m* /**la** *f* **plus** (most) or
le *m* /**la** *f* **moins** (least) before the adjective.

Example:

le vin sec	the dry wine
le vin plus sec	the drier wine
le vin le plus sec	the driest wine
la bague chère	the expensive ring
la bague moins chère	the less expensive ring
la bague la moins chère	the least expensive ring

Possessive Adjectives

Possessive adjectives come before the noun and must agree in gender and
number with the noun/object, not the person possessing the object.

	Masculine	Feminine	Plural
my	**mon**	**ma**	**mes**
your (sing.)	**ton**	**ta**	**tes**
his/her	**son**	**sa**	**ses**
our	**notre**	**notre**	**nos**
your (pl.)	**votre**	**votre**	**vos**
their	**leur**	**leur**	**leurs**

Example:

**Où sont nos passeports ? Cherchons dans mon sac et dans ta
valise.**

Where are our passports? Let's look in my purse and in your suitcase.

Adverbs & Adverbial Expressions

Adverbs describe verbs. They are often formed by adding **-ment** to the feminine form of the adjective.

Examples:

Nous prenons le train lent.	We are taking the slow train.
Jean conduit lentement.	Jean drives slowly.
Il prends la route rapide.	He is taking the fast route.
Frédérique conduit rapidement.	Frédérique drives fast.

Prepositions

Prepositions are paired with nouns or verbs to create descriptive phrases. In French, several important prepositions form contractions when they appear in front of certain other words.

Some/Any

To express how much of something (to eat, to buy, etc.), French uses a construction called the partitive. The partitive is similar to some or any in English, and it is formed by combining **de** with the definite article (**le, la** or **les**). Even if some or any is not explicit in English, the partitive is always used in French.

Examples:

de + la *f* (sing.) =	**Je voudrais de la soupe.**
de la	I'd like some soup.
de + le *m* (sing.) =	**Avez-vous commandé du fromage?**
du	Did you order any cheese?
de + l' (before a	**Nous avons commandé de l'eau.**
vowel) = **de l'**	We have ordered some water.
de + les (pl.) =	**Il achete des chaussures.**
des	He is buying shoes.

At/To

French expressions that use the word **à** are formed somewhat like the phrases using **de**.

Examples:

à + la *f* (sing.) =	**Je vais à la plage.**
à la	I am going to the beach.
à + le *m* (sing.) =	**Nous restons au musée.**
au	We're staying at the museum.
à + l' (before a	**Elles sont à l'église.**
vowel) = **à l'**	They are at the church.
à + les (pl.) =	**Ils vont aux États-Unis.**
aux	They are going to the United States.

Numbers

ESSENTIAL

0	**zéro**	*zay·roh*
1	**un**	*uhN*
2	**deux**	*duh*
3	**trois**	*trwah*
4	**quatre**	*kah·truh*
5	**cinq**	*sehNk*
6	**six**	*sees*
7	**sept**	*seht*
8	**huit**	*weet*
9	**neuf**	*nuhf*
10	**dix**	*dees*
11	**onze**	*ohNz*
12	**douze**	*dooz*

13	**treize** *trehz*
14	**quatorze** *kah·tohrz*
15	**quinze** *kehNz*
16	**seize** *sehz*
17	**dix-sept** *dee·seht*
18	**dix-huit** *deez·weet*
19	**dix-neuf** *deez·nuhf*
20	**vingt** *vehN*
21	**vingt-et-un** *vehN·tay·uhN*
22	**vingt-deux** *vehN·duh*
30	**trente** *trawNt*
31	**trente-et-un** *trawN·tay·uhN*
40	**quarante** *kah·rawNt*
50	**cinquante** *sehN·kawNt*
60	**soixante** *swah·zawNt*
70	**soixante-dix** *swah·zawNt·dees*
80	**quatre-vingt** *kah·truh·vehN*
90	**quatre-vingt-dix** *kah·truh·vehN·dees*
100	**cent** *sawN*
101	**cent-un** *sawN·uhN*
200	**deux-cent** *duh·sawN*
500	**cinq-cent** *sehNk·sawN*
1,000	**mille** *meel*
10,000	**dix mille** *dee meel*
1,000,000	**un million** *uhN meel·yohN*

Ordinal Numbers

first	**premier** *m* /**première** *f*
	pruh·meeyay/pruh·meeyehr
second	**deuxième** *duh·zeeyehm*

third	**troisième** *trwah·zeeyehm*
fourth	**quatrième** *kah·treeyehm*
fifth	**cinquième** *sehN·keeyehm*
once	**une fois** *ewn fwah*
twice	**deux fois** *duh fwah*
three times	**trois fois** *trwah fwah*

Time

ESSENTIAL

What time is it?	**Quelle heure est-il ?** *kehl uhr ay·teel*
It's midday.	**Il est midi.** *ee lay mee·dee*
At midnight.	**À minuit.** *ah mee·nwee*
From one o'clock	**D'une heure à deux heures.**
to two o'clock.	*dewn nuhr ah duh zuhr*
Five past three.	**Trois heures cinq.** *trwah zuhr sehNk*
A quarter to ten.	**Dix heures moins le quart.**
	dee zuhr mwehN luh kahr
5:30 a.m./p.m.	**Cinq heures et demie du matin/**
	de l'après-midi. *sehN kuhr eh duh·mee dew*
	mah·tehN/duh lah·preh·mee·dee

In France, the 24-hour clock is used for time, especially in schedules. The morning hours from 1:00 a.m. to noon are the same as in English. After that, just add 12 to the time: 1:00 p.m. would be 13:00, 5:00 p.m. would be 17:00 and so on. In ordinary conversation, time is generally expressed using the 12-hour clock, with the addition of **du matin** (morning/a.m.), **de l'après-midi** (afternoon) or **du soir** (evening/p.m.).

Days

ESSENTIAL

Monday	**lundi** *luhN•dee*
Tuesday	**mardi** *mahr•dee*
Wednesday	**mercredi** *mehr•kruh•dee*
Thursday	**jeudi** *zhuh•dee*
Friday	**vendredi** *vawN•druh•dee*
Saturday	**samedi** *sahm•dee*
Sunday	**dimanche** *dee•mawNsh*

Calendars in France are organized Monday to Sunday.

Dates

yesterday	**hier** *eeyehr*
today	**aujourd'hui** *oh•zhoor•dwee*
tomorrow	**demain** *duh•mehN*
day	**le jour** *luh zhoor*
week	**la semaine** *lah suh•mehN*
month	**le mois** *luh mwah*
year	**l'année/l'an** *lah•nay/lawN*

France follows a day-month-year format instead of the
month-day-year format used in the U.S.
E.g.: **le vingt-cinq juillet deux mille huit** = July 25, 2008;
25/07/08 = 7/25/2008

Months

January	**janvier** *zhawN•veeyay*
February	**février** *fay•vreeyay*

March	**mars** *mahrs*
April	**avril** *ah·vreel*
May	**mai** *may*
June	**juin** *zhwehN*
July	**juillet** *zhwee·yay*
August	**août** *oot*
September	**septembre** *sehp·tawN·bruh*
October	**octobre** *ohk·toh·bruh*
November	**novembre** *noh·vawN·bruh*
December	**décembre** *day·sawN·bruh*

Seasons

spring	**le printemps** *luh prehN·tawN*
summer	**l'été** *lay·tay*
autumn	**l'automne** *loh·tohNn*
winter	**l'hiver** *lee·vehr*

Public Holidays

January 1: New Year's Day, **Le Nouvel An**
May 1: Labor Day, **La Fête du Travail**
May 8: Victory Day, **La Fête de la Libération**
July 14: Bastille Day, **La Fête Nationale**
August 15: Assumption Day, **L'Assomption**
November 1: All Saints Day, **La Toussaint**
November 11: Armistice Day, **L'Armistice**
December 25: Christmas, **Noël**
Good Friday, **Le Vendredi Saint**
Easter, **Pâques**
Easter Monday, **Le Lundi de Pâques**
Ascension, **L'Ascension**
Pentecost, **La Pentecôte**

The most important public holiday is **La Fête Nationale** (Bastille Day) on July 14. This holiday symbolizes the victory of the revolutionaries over the monarchy in 1789, creating the basis for the French Republic. **La Marseillaise**, the French national anthem, was created during the French Revolution, along with France's motto: **Liberté, Égalité, Fraternité** (Liberty, Equality, Brotherhood). The evening before July 14, people go to cafes and improvised dance areas; it is a festive atmosphere with dancing and celebration. There are firework displays throughout France that evening and on the 14th. The French president and members of the government, as well as other dignitaries, attend the **défilé**, a large military parade, on the Champs Élysées on Bastille Day.

Conversion Tables

When you know	Multiply by	To find
ounces	28.3	grams
pounds	0.45	kilograms
inches	2.54	centimeters
feet	0.3	meters
miles	1.61	kilometers
square inches	6.45	sq. centimeters
square feet	0.09	sq. meters
square miles	2.59	sq. kilometers
pints (U.S./Brit)	0.47/0.56	liters
gallons (U.S./Brit)	3.8/4.5	liters
Fahrenheit	5/9, after 32	Centigrade
Centigrade	9/5, then +32	Fahrenheit

Kilometers to Miles Conversions

1 km	0.62 miles
5 km	3.1 miles
10 km	6.2 miles
50 km	31 miles
100 km	62 miles

Measurement

1 gram	**un gramme** *uhN grahm*	= 1000 milligrams	= 0.035oz.
1 kilogram (kg)	**un kilo(gramme)** *uhN kee·loh (grahm)*	= 1000 grams	= 2.2 lb
1 liter (l)	**un litre** *uhN lee·truh*	= 1000 milliliters	= 1.06 U.S/ 0.88 Brit Quarts
1 centimeter	**un centimètre** *uhN sawN·tee·meh·truh*	= 10 millimeters	= 0.4 inch (cm)
1 meter (m)	**un mètre** *uhN meh·truh*	= 100 centimeters	= 39.37 inches/ 3.28 ft.
1 kilometer	**un kilomètre** *uhN kee·loh·meh·truh*	= 1000 meters	= 0.62 mile (km)

Temperature

-40°C – -40°F	**-1°C** – 30°F	**20°C** – 68°F
-30°C – -22°F	**0°C** – 32°F	**25°C** – 77°F
-20°C – -4°F	**5°C** – 41°F	**30°C** – 86°F
-10°C – 14°F	**10°C** – 50°F	**35°C** – 95°F
-5°C – 23°F	**15°C** – 59°F	

Oven Temperature

100°C – 212°F	**177°C** – 350°F
121°C – 250°F	**204°C** – 400°F
149°C – 300°F	**260°C** – 500°F

English–French 181
French–English 203

Dictionary

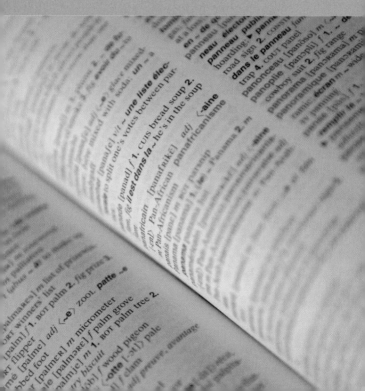

English–French

A

abbey l'abbaye
accept v accepter
access v accéder; n accès
accident l'accident
accommodation le logement
account le compte
acetaminophen le paracétamol
acupuncture l'acupuncture
adapter l'adaptateur
address l'adresse
admission l'entrée
after après; ~**noon** l'après-midi;
  ~**shave** l'après-rasage
age l'âge
agency l'agence
AIDS Déficience le Syndrome
  d'immunodéficience acquise
air l'air; ~ **conditioning** la
  climatisation; ~ **pump** la pompe
  à air; ~**line** la compagnie
  aérienne; ~**mail** par avion;
  ~**plane** l'avion; ~**port** l'aéroport
aisle (plane) le couloir;
  ~ **(theater)** l'allée; ~ **seat** le
  siège couloir
allergic allergique; ~ **reaction**
  la -réaction allergique
allow v permettre

alone seul
alter v modifier
aluminum foil le papier aluminium
amazing surprenant
ambulance l'ambulance
American américain
amusement park le parc
  d'attractions
and et
anemic anémique
anesthesia l'anesthésie
animal l'animal
ankle la cheville
antibiotic l'antibiotique
antiques store l'antiquaire
antiseptic cream la crème
  antiseptique
anything rien
apartment l'appartement
appendix (body part) l'appendice
appetizer l'entrée
appointment le rendez-vous
arcade la salle de jeux
area code le code régional
arm le bras
aromatherapy l'aromathérapie
around (the corner) au coin
arrivals (airport) les arrivées
arrive v arriver

adj adjective	**BE** British English	**v** verb
adv adverb	**n** noun	

artery l'artère
arthritis l'arthrite
art l'art
Asian asiatique
aspirin l'aspirine
asthmatic asthmatique
ATM le distributeur automatique de billets; ~ **card** la carte de retrait
attack l'attaque
attend v participer
attraction (place) le lieu touristique
attractive beau
Australia l'Australie
Australian australien
automatic automatique; ~ **car** la voiture automatique
available disponible

B

baby le bébé; ~ **bottle** le biberon; ~ **wipe** la lingette pour bébé; ~**sitter** le baby-sitter
back (body part) le dos; ~**ache** le mal de dos; ~**pack** le sac à dos
bag le sac
baggage [BE] le bagage; ~ **claim** le -retrait des bagages; ~ **ticket** l'étiquette
bakery la boulangerie
ballet le ballet
bandage le pansement
bank la banque
bar (place) le bar
barbecue le barbecue

barber le coiffeur pour hommes
baseball le baseball
basket (grocery store) le panier
basketball le basketball
bathroom la salle de bains
battery la pile
battleground le champ de bataille
be v être
beach la plage
beautiful beau
bed le lit; ~ **and breakfast** le bed and breakfast
before avant
begin v commencer
beginner le débutant
behind derrière
beige beige
belt la ceinture
berth la couchette
best meilleur
better mieux
bicycle la bicyclette; le vélo
big grand ~ **bigger** plus grand
bike route la piste cyclable
bikini le bikini; ~ **wax** l'épilation à la cire du maillot
bill (charge) v facturer; ~ n **(invoice)** la facture; ~ n **(money)** la coupure; ~ n **(of sale)** le reçu
bird l'oiseau
birthday l'anniversaire
black noir
bladder la vessie
bland sans goût
blanket la couverture

bleed v saigner
blood le sang; ~ **pressure** la tension
blouse le chemisier
blue bleu
board v embarquer; ~**ing pass** la carte d'embarquement
boat le bateau
bone l'os
book le livre; ~**store** la librairie
boots les bottes
boring ennuyant
botanical garden le jardin botanique
bother v ennuyer
bottle la bouteille; ~ **opener** l'ouvre-bouteille
bowl le saladier
box la boîte
boxing match le match de boxe
boy le garçon; ~**friend** le petit-ami
bra le soutien-gorge
bracelet le bracelet
brakes (car) les freins
break v (tooth/bone) casser
breakdown la panne
breakfast le petit déjeuner
break-in (burglary) l'effraction
breast le sein; ~**feed** v allaiter
breathe v respirer
bridge pont
briefs (clothing) les slips
bring v apporter
British anglais
broken cassé
brooch la broche

broom le balai
brother le frère
brown marron
bug l'insecte
building le bâtiment
burn v brûler
bus le bus; ~ **station** la gare routière; ~ **stop** l'arrêt de bus; ~ **ticket** le ticket de bus; ~ **tour** la visite en bus
business les affaires; ~ **card** la carte de visite; ~ **center** le centre d'affaires; ~ **class** la classe affaire; ~ **hours** les heures d'ouverture
butcher le boucher
buttocks les fesses
buy v acheter
bye au revoir

C

cabaret le cabaret
cabin la cabine
cable car le téléphérique
café le café
call v appeler; ~ **collect** appeler ~ n l'appel en PCV;
calories les kilocalories
camera l'appareil photo; ~ **case** le sac à appareil photo; ~ **store** la boutique photo
camp v camper; ~**ing stove** le réchaud; ~**site** le camping
can opener le l'ouvre-boîte
Canada le Canada
Canadian canadien

cancel *v* annuler
candy le bonbon
canned goods les conserves
canyon la gorge
car la voiture; ~ **hire** [BE] la voiture de location; ~ **park** [BE] le parking; **rental**
~ la voiture de location;
~ **seat** le siège bébé
carafe la carafe
card la carte; **ATM** ~ la carte de retrait; **credit** ~ la carte de crédit; **phone** ~ le carte de téléphone
carry-on (piece of hand luggage) le bagage à main
cart le chariot
carton le paquet; ~ **of cigarettes** la cartouche de cigarettes
case (amount) le cas
cash *v* encaisser; ~ *n* le liquide; ~ **advance** l'avance
cashier la caisse
casino le casino
castle le château
cathedral la cathédrale
cave la grotte
CD le CD (disque compact)
cell phone le portable
Celsius Celsius
centimeter le centimètre
certificate le certificat
chair la chaise; ~ **lift** le télésiège
change *v* **(baby)** changer; ~ **(money)** échanger;

~ *n* **(money)** la monnaie;
charcoal le charbon de bois
charge *v* **(credit card)** payer par carte
charge (cost) le coût
cheap bon marché
cheaper moins cher
check *v* **(luggage)** enregistrer; ~ **(on something)** vérifier; ~ *n* **(payment)** le chèque; ~-**in (hotel/airport)** l'enregistrement; ~**ing account** le compte courant; ~-**out (hotel)** quitter la chambre
Cheers! Santé!
chemical toilet les toilettes portables
chemist [BE] la pharmacie
cheque [BE] le chèque
chest (body part) la poitrine; ~ **pain** la douleur à la poitrine
chewing gum le chewing-gum
child l'enfant; ~'**s seat** le siège enfant
children's menu le menu enfant
children's portion la portion enfant
chopsticks les baguettes
church l'église
cigar le cigare
cigarette la cigarette
class la classe
classical music la musique classique
clean *v* nettoyer; ~ *adj* propre; ~**ing product** le produit d'entretien; ~**ing supplies**

les produits d'entretien
clear v **(on an ATM)** effacer
cliff la falaise
cling film [BE] le cellophane
close v **(shop)** fermer;
~ adv près; **~d** fermé
clothing les vêtements;
~ **store** le magasin de vêtements
club le club
coat le manteau
coffee shop le café
coin la pièce
colander la passoire
cold (sickness) le rhume;
~ **(temperature)** froid
colleague le collègue
cologne l'eau de Cologne
color la couleur
comb le peigne
come v venir
complaint la plainte
computer l'ordinateur
concert le concert; ~ **hall**
la salle de concert
condition (medical)
l'état de santé
conditioner l'après-shampooing
condom le préservatif
conference la conférence
confirm v confirmer
congestion la congestion
connect v **(internet)**
se connecter
connection (flight)
la correspondance;
~ **(internet)** la connexion

constipated constipé
consulate le consulat
consultant le consultant
contact v contacter
contact lens les lentilles de
contact; ~ **solution**
la solution pour lentilles
de contact
contagious contagieux
convention hall le palais des
congrès
conveyor belt le carrousel
cook v cuisiner; **~ing gas**
le gaz
cool (temperature) frais
copper le cuivre
corkscrew le tire-bouchon
cost v coûter
cot le lit pliant
cotton le coton
cough v tousser; ~ n la toux
country code le code national
cover charge (bar, club) le droit
d'entrée; ~ **(restaurant)**
le couvert
crash v **(car)** avoir un
accident
cream (ointment) la crème
credit card la carte de crédit
crew neck le col rond
crib le berceau
crystal le cristal
cup la tasse
currency la monnaie;
~ **exchange** l'échange de
monnaie; ~ **exchange office**

le bureau de change
current account [BE] le compte courant
customs la douane
cut v couper; ~ n **(injury)** la coupure
cute mignon
cycling faire du vélo

D

damage v abîmer; **~d** endommagé
dance v danser; ~ **club** la discothèque; **~ing** dansant
dangerous dangereux
dark sombre
date (calendar) la date
day le jour
deaf sourd
debit card la carte de retrait
deck chair la chaise longue
declare v déclarer
decline v **(credit card)** refuser
deeply profondément
degree (temperature) le degré
delay v retarder
delete v **(computer)** supprimer
delicatessen la charcuterie
delicious délicieux
denim jean
dentist le dentiste
denture le dentier
deodorant le déodorant
department store le grand magasin
departures (airport) les départs
deposit v déposer; ~ **(bank)** le dépôt

desert le désert
detergent le détergent
develop v **(film)** développer
diabetic diabétique
dial v composer
diamond le diamant
diaper la couche
diarrhea la diarrhée
diesel le gazole
difficult difficile
digital numérique; ~ **camera** l'appareil photo numérique; ~ **photo** la photo numérique
dining room la salle à manger
dinner le dîner
direction la direction
dirty sale
disabled [BE] handicapé; ~ **accessible [BE]** accessible aux handicapés
disconnect v **(computer)** déconnecter
discount la réduction
dish (kitchen) la vaisselle; **~washer** le lave-vaisselle; **~washing liquid** le détergent pour lave-vaisselle
display montrer; ~ **case** la vitrine
disposable jetable; ~ **razor** le rasoir jetable
dive v plonger; **~ing equipment** l'équipement de plongée
divorce v divorcer
dizzy avoir des vertiges
doctor le docteur
doll la poupée

dollar (U.S.) le dollar
domestic national;
~ **flight** le vol national
door la porte
dormitory le dortoir
double bed le lit double
downtown (direction) vers
le centre-ville; ~ **area**
le centre-ville
dozen la douzaine
drag lift le remonte-pentes
dress (piece of clothing)
la robe; ~ **code** la tenue
exigée
drink v boire; ~ n la boisson;
~ **menu** la carte des boissons
drinking water l'eau potable
drive v conduire; ~**r's license**
number le numéro de permis
de conduire
drop (medicine) la goutte
drowsiness la somnolence
dry cleaner la teinturerie
dubbed doublé
during pendant
duty (tax) la taxe
duty-free hors taxe
DVD DVD

E

ear l'oreille; ~**ache** l'otite
early tôt
earrings les boucles d'oreille
east est
easy facile
eat v manger

economy class la classe économique
elbow le coude
electric outlet la prise électrique
elevator l'ascenseur
e-mail v envoyer un mail;
~ n le mail; ~ **address** l'adresse
mail
emergency l'urgence; ~ **exit**
la sortie de secours
empty v vider
enamel (jewelry) l'émail
end v finir
English anglais
engrave v graver
enjoy v prendre plaisir
enter v entrer
entertainment le divertissement
entrance l'entrée
envelope l'enveloppe
equipment l'équipement
escalators l'escalator
e-ticket le billet électronique
EU resident le résident européen
euro l'euro
evening la soirée
excess l'excès
exchange v échanger; ~ n
(place) le bureau de change;
~ **rate** le taux de change
excursion l'excursion
excuse v excuser
exhausted épuisé
exit v sortir; ~ n la sortie
expensive cher
expert (skill level) l'expert
exposure (film) la pose

express express; ~ **bus**
le bus direct; ~ **train**
l'express
extension (phone) le poste
extra extra; ~ **large** très grand
extract v **(tooth)** arracher
eye l'œil
eyebrow wax l'épilation à la cire des
sourcils

F

face le visage
facial le soin du visage
family la famille
fan (appliance) le ventilateur;
~ **(souvenir)** l'éventail
far loin
farm la ferme
far-sighted presbyte
fast vite; ~ **food** le fast food
faster plus vite
fat free 0% de matières
grasses
father le père
fax v envoyer un fax; ~ n le fax;
~ **number** le numéro de fax
feed v nourrir
ferry le ferry
fever la fièvre
field (sports) le terrain de
sport
fill v faire le plein
fill v **out (form)** remplir
filling (tooth) le plombage
film (camera) la pellicule
fine (fee for breaking law)
la contravention

finger le doigt; ~**nail** l'ongle
fire le feu; ~ **department** les
pompiers; ~ **door** la porte
coupe-feu
first premier; ~ **class**
la première classe
fitting room la cabine
d'essayage
fix v **(repair)** réparer
flashlight la lampe torche
flat tire [tyre BE] le pneu crevé
flight le vol
floor le sol
flower la fleur
folk music la musique folklorique
food la nourriture
foot le pied
football [BE] le football;
~ **game [BE]** le match de football
for pour
forecast la météo
forest la forêt
fork la fourchette
form le formulaire
formula (baby) le lait pour bébés
fort le fort
fountain la fontaine
France la France
free libre
freezer le congélateur
French français
fresh frais
friend l'ami
frying pan la poêle
full-service le service complet
full-time le temps plein

G

game le match
garage le garage
garbage bag le sac poubelle
gas l'essence; ~ **station** la station
service
gate (airport) la porte
gay gay; ~ **bar** le bar gay;
~ **club** le club gay
gel (hair) le gel
get off v (a train, bus, subway)
descendre
get to v aller
gift le cadeau; ~ **shop** la boutique
cadeaux
girl la fille; ~friend la petite-amie
give v donner
glass le verre;
glasses les lunettes
go v (somewhere) aller
gold l'or
golf course le terrain de golf
golf tournament le tournoi de golf
good adj bon; ~ n le produit;
~ **afternoon** bon après-midi;
~ **evening** bonsoir; ~ morning
bonjour; ~**bye** au revoir
goods les produits
gram le gramme
grandchild les petits-enfants
grandparent les grands-parents
gray gris
green vert
grocery store le magasin de fruits
et légumes
ground floor le rez-de-chaussée

groundcloth le tapis de sol
groundsheet le drap du dessous
group le groupe
guide le guide; ~ **book**
le guide; ~ **dog** le chien d'aveugle
gym la gym
gynecologist le gynécologue

H

hair les cheveux; dryer
le sèche-cheveux d'étudiant;
~ **salon** le coiffeur; ~**brush**
la brosse; ~**cut** la coupe de
cheveux; ~**spray** la laque;
~**style** le style de coiffure;
~**stylist** le coiffeur
half la moitié; ~ **hour**
la demi-heure ~-**kilo**
le demi-kilo
hammer le marteau
hand la main; ~ **luggage** [BE]
le bagage à main; ~**bag** [BE]
le sac à main
handicapped l'handicapé;
~-**accessible** accessible aux
handicapés
hangover la gueule
de bois
happy heureux
hat le chapeau
have v avoir
head (body part) la tête;
~**ache** le mal de tête;
~**phones** les écouteurs
health la santé; ~ **food store**
le magasin de produits

diététiques
heart le cœur; **~ condition**
le problème cardiaque
heat le chauffage; **~er**
le chauffage
hectare l'hectare
hello bonjour
helmet le casque
help v aider; **~** n l'aide
here ici
hi salut
high haut; **~chair** la chaise haute;
~-heeled shoes les chaussures à
talons aiguilles; **~way** l'autoroute
hiking boots les chaussures de
marche
hill la colline
hire v [BE] louer; **~ car** [BE]
la voiture de location
hitchhike v faire de l'auto-stop
hockey le hockey
holiday [BE] les vacances
horsetrack le champ de course
hospital l'hôpital
hostel l'auberge de jeunesse
hot (spicy) épicé;
~ (temperature) chaud;
~ spring la source chaude;
~ water l'eau chaude
hotel l'hôtel
hour l'heure
house la maison; **~hold goods**
les produits ménagers; **~keeping
service** le service d'entretien
how comment; **~ much** combien
hug v enlacer

hungry faim
hurt la douleur
husband le mari

I

ibuprofen l'ibuprofène
ice la glace; **~ hockey**
le hockey sur glace
icy glacé
identification l'identification
ill malade
in dans
include v inclure
indoor pool la piscine intérieure
inexpensive pas cher
infected infecté
information (phone) les
renseignements; **~ desk**
le bureau des renseignements
insect l'insecte; **~ bite**
la piqûre d'insecte; **~ repellent**
la lotion anti-insectes
insert v insérer
insomnia l'insomnie
instant message le message
instantané
insulin l'insuline
insurance l'assurance;
~ card la carte d'assurance;
~ company la compagnie
d'assurance
interesting intéressant
intermediate le niveau
intermédiaire
international (airport area)
l'international (terminal);

~ **flight** le vol international;
~ **student card** la carte
internationale d'étudiant
internet l'internet; ~ **cafe**
le cyber café; ~ **service**
le service internet
interpreter l'interprète
intersection l'intersection
intestine l'intestin
introduce v présenter
invoice [BE] la facture
Ireland l'Irlande
Irish irlandais
iron v repasser;
~ n (**clothes**) le fer à
repasser
Italian italien

J

jacket la veste
jar le pot
jaw la mâchoire
jazz le jazz; ~ **club** le club de
jazz
jeans le jean
jet ski le jet ski
jeweler la bijouterie
jewelry le bijou
join v joindre
joint (body part) l'articulation

K

key la clé; ~ **card** la carte de la
chambre; ~ **ring** la chaîne
kiddie pool la pataugeoire
kidney (body part) le rein

kilo le kilo; ~**gram** le
kilogramme; ~**meter** le
kilomètre
kiss v embrasser
kitchen la cuisine; ~ **foil [BE]**
le papier aluminium
knee le genou
knife le couteau

L

lace la dentelle
lactose intolerant allergique au
lactose
lake le lac
large grand
larger plus grand
last dernier
late (time) tard
later plus tard
laundromat
la laverie automatique
laundry la lessive; ~ **facility**
la buanderie; ~ **service** le service
de nettoyage
lawyer l'avocat
leather le cuir
leave v partir
left (direction) à gauche
leg la jambe
lens le verre
less moins
lesson la leçon
letter la lettre
library la bibliothèque
life jacket le gilet de
sauvetage

lifeguard le secouriste
lift [BE] l'ascenseur; ~ **pass** le forfait
light (cigarette) v allumer; ~ adj **(overhead)** blond; ~**bulb** l'ampoule
lighter le briquet
like v aimer
line (train) la ligne
linen le lin
lip les lèvres
liquor store le marchand de vins et de spiritueux
liter le litre
little adv peu; ~ adj petit
live v vivre
liver (body part) le foie
loafers les mocassins
local du quartier
lock v fermer; ~ n le cadenas; ~**er** la consigne
log off (computer) terminer une session
log on (computer) ouvrir une session
long long; ~ **sleeves** les manches longues; ~**-sighted** [BE] presbyte
look v regarder
lose v **(something)** perdre
lost perdu; ~ **and found** les objets trouvés
lotion la crème
louder plus fort
love v **(someone)** aimer; ~ n amour
low bas

luggage le bagage; ~ **cart** le chariot; ~ **locker** la consigne; ~ **ticket** le retrait des bagages
lunch le déjeuner
lung le poumon

M

magazine le magazine
magnificent magnifique
mail le courrier; ~**box** la boîte-à-lettres
main attraction la principale attraction touristique
main course le plat principal
mall le centre commercial
man l'homme
manager le responsable
manicure la manucure
manual car la voiture manuelle
map la carte
market le marché
married marié
marry v se marier
mass (church service) la messe
massage le massage
match le match
meal le repas
measure v **(someone)** mesurer
measuring cup la mesure
measuring spoon la cuillère à doser
mechanic le mécanicien
medicine le médicament
medium (size) moyen
meet v **(someone)** rencontrer
meeting la réunion; ~ **room** la salle de réunion

membership card la carte de membre
memorial (place) le lieu commémoratif
memory card la carte mémoire
mend v raccourcir
menstrual cramp les règles douloureuses
menu la carte
message le message
meter (parking) l'horodateur
microwave le micro-onde
midday [BE] midi
midnight minuit
mileage le kilométrage
mini-bar le mini bar
minute la minute
missing disparu
mistake l'erreur
mobile home le mobile home
mobile phone [BE] le portable
mobility la mobilité
money l'argent
month le mois
mop la serpillière
moped la mobylette
more plus
morning le matin
mosque la mosquée
mother la mère
motion sickness (air) le mal de l'air; ~ **(sea)** le mal de mer
motor boat le bateau à moteur
motorcycle la mobylette
motorway [BE] l'autoroute
mountain la montagne

mousse la mousse
mouth la bouche
movie le film; ~ **theater** le cinéma
mug v attaquer
muscle le muscle
museum le musée
music la musique; ~ **store** le disquaire

N

nail file la lime á ongle
nail salon l'onglerie
name le nom
napkin la serviette
nappies [BE] les couches
nationality la nationalité
nature preserve la réserve naturelle
nausea la nausée
near près; ~**by** près de; ~**-sighted** myope
neck le cou
necklace le collier
need v avoir besoin
newspaper le journal
newsstand le kiosque à journaux
next suivant
nice bien
night la nuit
nightclub le night club
no non
non-alcoholic non alcoolisé
non-smoking non fumeur
noon midi
north nord

nose le nez
note [BE] la coupure
nothing rien
notify *v* informer
novice (skill level) novice
now maintenant
number le nombre; le numéro
nurse l'infirmier

O

office le bureau; **~ hours** les heures d'ouverture
off-licence [BE] le marchand de vins et de spiritueux
oil l'huile
OK d'accord
old vieux
on the corner au coin
once une fois
one un; **~-way (ticket)** l'aller simple; **~-way street** le sens unique
only seulement
open *v* ouvrir; **~** adj ouvert
opera l'opéra; **~ house** l'opéra
opposite le contraire
optician l'opticien
orange (color) orange
orchestra l'orchestre
order v commander
outdoor pool la piscine extérieure
outside dehors
over-the-counter (medication) sans ordonnance
overlook (scenic place) le point d'observation

overnight de nuit
oxygen treatment le soin à l'oxygène

P

pacifier la tétine
pack *v* faire les bagages
package le colis
pad [BE] la serviette hygiénique
pain la douleur
pajamas le pyjama
palace le palais
panties les culottes
pants le pantalon
pantyhose le collant
paper le papier; **~ towel** la serviette en papier
paracetamol [BE] le paracétamol
park *v* se garer; **~** *n* le parc; **~ing garage** le garage; **~ing lot** le parking
part (for car) la pièce; **~-time** le temps partiel
pass through v passer
passenger le passager
passport le passeport; **~ control** le contrôle de passeport
password le mot de passe
pastry shop la pâtisserie
path le chemin
pay *v* payer; **~ phone** le téléphone public
peak (of a mountain) le sommet
pearl la perle

pedestrian le piéton
pediatrician le pédiatre
pedicure la pédicure
pen le stylo
penicillin la pénicilline
penis le pénis
per par; **~ day** par jour; **~ hour** par heure; **~ night** par nuit; **~ week** par semaine
perfume le parfum
period (menstrual) les règles; **~ (of time)** la période
permit v permettre
personal identification number (PIN) le code secret
petite menue
petrol [BE] le l'essence; **~ station [BE]** la station service
pewter l'étain
pharmacy la pharmacie
phone v téléphoner; **~ n** le téléphone; **~ call** l'appel; **~ card** la carte de téléphone; **~ number** le numéro de téléphone
photo la photo; **~copy** la photocopie; **~graphy** la photographie
pick up v (something) prendre
picnic area l'aire de pique-nique
piece le morceau
Pill (birth control) la pilule
pillow l'oreiller
pink rose
piste [BE] la piste; **~ map [BE]** la carte des pistes

pizzeria la pizzeria
place v (a bet) parier
plane l'avion
plastic wrap le cellophane
plate l'assiette
platform le quai
platinum platine
play v jouer; **~ n** (theater) la pièce **~ground** l'aire de jeux **~pen** le parc
please s'il vous plaît
pleasure le plaisir
plunger le déboucheur de toilettes
plus size grande taille
pocket la poche
poison le poison
poles (skiing) les bâtons
police la police; **~ report** le rapport de police; **~ station** le commissariat de police
pond l'étang
pool la piscine
pop music la pop musique
portion la portion
post [BE] le courrier; **~ office** le bureau de poste; **~box [BE]** la boîte-à-lettres; **~card** la carte postale
pot la casserole
pottery la poterie
pound (British sterling) la livre sterling
pregnant enceinte
prescribe v prescrire
prescription l'ordonnance

press v (clothing) repasser
price le prix
print v imprimer
problem le problème
produce v produire;
~ **store** le marchand de fruits et légumes
prohibit v interdire
pronounce v prononcer
public public
pull v (door sign) tirer
purple pourpre
purse le sac
push v (door sign) pousser
pushchair [BE] la poussette

Q

quality la qualité
question la question
quiet le silence; le calme

R

racetrack la piste de courses
racket (sports) la raquette
railway station [BE] la gare
rain la pluie; ~**coat** l'imperméable;
~**forest** la forêt vierge
rainy pluvieux
rap (music) le rap
rape v violer; ~ n le viol
rash l'irritation cutanée
razor blade la lame de rasoir
reach v atteindre
ready prêt
real vrai
receipt le reçu

receive v recevoir
reception la réception
recharge v recharger
recommend v recommander
recommendation la recommandation
recycling les ordures à recycler
red rouge
refrigerator le réfrigérateur
region la région
registered mail le courrier recommandé
regular ordinaire
relationship la relation
rent v louer; ~**al car** la voiture de location
repair v réparer
repeat v répéter
reservation la réservation;
~ **desk** le bureau de réservation
reserve v réserver
restaurant le restaurant
restroom les toilettes
retired v prendre sa retraite
return v (something) rendre;
~ n [BE] l'aller-retour
rib (body part) la côte
right (direction) à droite;
~ **of way** le droit de passage
ring la bague
river la rivière
road map la carte routière
rob v voler
romantic romantique

room la pièce; ~ **key** la clé;
~ **service** le service de chambre
round-trip l'aller-retour
route la route
rowboat la barque
rubbish [BE] les poubelles;
~ **bag [BE]** le sac poubelle
rugby le rugby
ruins les ruines

S

sad triste
safe adj en sécurité;
~ n le coffre-fort
sales tax la TVA
same le même
sandals les sandales
sanitary napkin la serviette
hygiénique
saucepan la casserole
sauna le sauna
save v **(computer)** sauvegarder
savings (account) le compte
épargne
scanner scanner
scarf l'écharpe
schedule v prévoir;
~ n l'horaire
science la science
scissors les ciseaux
sea la mer
seat le siège
security la sécurité
see v voir
self-service le self-service
sell v vendre

seminar le séminaire
send v envoyer
senior citizens les seniors
separated (marriage)
séparés
serious sérieux
service (in a restaurant)
le service
**sexually transmitted disease
(STD)** les maladies sexuellement
transmissibles
shampoo le shampooing
sharp tranchant
shaving cream la mousse à raser
sheet le drap
shirt la chemise
ship v envoyer
shoe store le magasin de chaussures
shoes les chaussures
shop v faire des achats
shopping les courses;
~ **area** le quartier des magasins;
~ **centre [BE]**
le centre commercial; ~ **mall**
le centre commercial
short court; ~-**sighted**
[BE] myope; ~ **sleeves**
les manches courtes; ~**s**
le short
shoulder l'épaule
show v montrer
shower la douche
shrine le lieu saint
sick malade
side dish l'accompagnement
side effect l'effet secondaire

sightseeing le tourisme;
~ **tour** la visite touristique
sign v signer
silk la soie
single (unmarried) adj célibataire;
n ~ **bed** le lit une place;
~ **prints** le tirage unique;
~ **room** la chambre simple
sink l'évier
sister la sœur
sit v s'asseoir
size la taille
ski v skier; ~ n le ski;
~ **lift** le télésiège
skin la peau
skirt la jupe
sleep v dormir
sleeper car le wagon
couchette
sleeping bag le sac de couchage
sleeping car [BE] le wagon
couchette
slice la tranche
slippers les chaussons
slower plus lent
slowly lentement
small petit
smaller plus petit
smoke v fumer
smoking (area) la zone
fumeur
snack bar le bar
sneakers les tennis
snorkeling equipment
l'équipement de plongée
snowboard le snowboard

snowshoe la chaussure de ski
snowy neigeux
soap le savon
soccer le football; ~ **game**
le match de football
sock la chaussette
soother [BE] la tétine
sore throat le mal de gorge
sorry désolé
south sud
souvenir le souvenir; ~ **store**
le magasin de souvenirs
spa le spa
spatula la spatule
speak v parler
special (food) la spécialité; le plat
typique
specialist (doctor)
le spécialiste
specimen l'échantillon
speed (velocity) la vitesse
spell v épeler
spicy épicé
spine (body part) la colonne
vertébrale
spoon la cuillère
sporting goods store
le magasin de sport
sports le sport; ~ **massage**
le massage sportif
sprain l'entorse
stadium le stade
stairs les escaliers
stamp v (a ticket) timbrer;
~ n (postage) le timbre
start v (a car) démarrer; v

(to begin) commencer
starter [BE] l'entrée
station la station; **~ wagon**
le break; **bus ~** la gare routière;
gas ~ la station service; muster
~ [BE] la salle d'attente; **petrol**
~ [BE] la station service; **subway**
~ la station de métro; **train ~** la
gare
statue la statue
stay v rester
steal v voler
steep escarpé
sterling silver l'argent fin
sting la piqûre
stolen volé
stomach l'estomac; **~ache** les
maux de ventre
stop v arrêter; **~** n l'arrêt
store directory le plan du magasin
stove la gazinière
straight droit
strange étrange
stream le ruisseau
stroller la poussette
student l'étudiant
study v étudier
stunning stupéfiant
subtitle subtil
subway le métro; **~ station**
la station de métro
suit le costume; **~case**
la valise
sun le soleil; **~ block** l'écran
solaire; **~burn** le coup de soleil;
~glasses les lunettes de soleil

sunny ensoleillé
sunscreen la crème solaire
sunstroke l'insolation
super (fuel) le super; **~market** le
supermarché; **~vision** la
supervision
surfboard le surf
swallow v avaler
sweater le pull
sweatshirt le sweat-shirt
sweet (taste) sucré
sweets [BE] les bonbons
swell v gonfler
swim v nager
swimsuit le maillot de bain
symbol (keyboard)
le symbole
synagogue la synagogue

T

table la table
tablet (medicine) le cachet
take v prendre
take away [BE] à emporter
tampon le tampon
taste v goûter
taxi le taxi
team l'équipe
teaspoon la cuillère à café
telephone le téléphone
temple (religious) le temple
temporary temporaire
tennis le tennis
tent la tente; **~ peg** le piquet;
~ pole le pilier
terminal (airport) le terminal

terracotta la terre cuite
terrible terrible
text v (**send a message**) écrire;
~ n (**message**) le texte
thank v remercier; ~ **you** merci
that ça/cela
theater le théâtre
theft le vol
there là
thief le voleur
thigh la cuisse
thirsty soif
this ceci
throat la gorge
ticket le billet; ~ **office** la
billetterie
tie (**clothing**) la cravate
time le temps; ~**table** [BE] les
horaires
tire [**tyre** BE] le pneu
tired fatigué
tissues les Kleenex
to go aller
tobacconist le tabac
today aujourd'hui
toe l'orteil; ~**nail** l'ongle
toilet [BE] les toilettes;
~ **paper** le papier toilette
tomorrow demain
tongue la langue
tonight ce soir
too trop
tooth la dent; ~**paste**
le dentifrice
total (**amount**) le total
tough (**food**) dur

tour la visite
tourist le touriste;
~ **information office**
le syndicat d'initiative
tow truck la dépanneuse
towel la serviette
tower la tour
town la ville; ~ **hall** la mairie;
~ **map** la carte de la ville;
~ **square** le centre ville
toy le jouet; ~ **store** le magasin de
jouets
track (**train**) le quai
traditional traditionnel
traffic light le feu tricolore
trail la piste; ~ **map** la carte des
pistes
trailer la remorque
train le train; ~ **station** la gare
translate v traduire
trash les poubelles
travel v voyager; ~ **agency**
l'agence de voyage; ~ **sickness**
le mal des transports; ~**er's check**
[**cheque** BE] le chèque de voyages
tree l'arbre
trim (**hair cut**) v égaliser
trip le voyage
trolley [BE] le chariot
trousers [BE] le pantalon
T-shirt le t-shirt
turn off v (**lights**) éteindre
turn on v (**lights**) allumer
TV la télé
type v taper

U

ugly laid
umbrella le parapluie
unattended sans surveillance
unbranded medication [BE] le médicament générique
unconscious inconscient
underground [BE] le métro; **~ station [BE]** la station de métro
underpants [BE] les slips
understand v comprendre
underwear les sous-vêtements
United Kingdom (U.K.) le Royaume Uni
United States (U.S.) les États-Unis
university l'université
unleaded (gas) sans plomb
upper supérieur
urgent urgent
use v utiliser
username le nom de l'utilisateur
utensil l'ustensile

V

vacancy libre
vacation les vacances
vaccination la vaccination
vacuum cleaner l'aspirateur
vagina le vagin
vaginal infection l'infection vaginale
valid valide
valley la vallée
valuable précieux
value la valeur

VAT [BE] la TVA
vegetarian végétarien
vehicle registration la carte grise
viewpoint [BE] le point d'observation
village le village
vineyard le vignoble
visit v visiter; **~ing hours** les heures de visite
visually impaired le malvoyant
vitamin la vitamine
V-neck le col en V
volleyball game le match de volleyball
vomit v vomir

W

wait v attendre; **~** n l'attente
waiter le serveur
waiting room la salle d'attente
waitress la serveuse
wake v réveiller; **~-up call** n l'appel réveil
walk v marcher; **~** n la promenade; **~ing route** le chemin de randonnée
wall clock la pendule
wallet le portefeuille
warm (something) v réchauffer **~** adj **(temperature)** chaud
washing machine la machine à laver
watch la montre

water skis les skis nautiques
waterfall la cascade
weather le temps
week la semaine; **~week-end** le week-end
weekly hebdomadaire
welcome v accueillir
well-rested bien reposé
west ouest
what quoi
wheelchair la chaise roulante; **~ ramp** la rampe d'accès
when quand
where où
white blanc; **~ gold** l'or blanc
who qui
widow le veuf
wife l'épouse
window la fenêtre; **~ case** le chambranle
windsurfer le véliplanchiste
wine list la carte des vins
wireless internet l'accès Wi-Fi

wireless phone le portable
with avec
withdraw v retirer
withdrawal (bank) le retrait
without sans
woman la femme
wool la laine
work v travailler
wrap v emballer
wrist le poignet
write v écrire

Y

year l'année
yellow jaune; **~ gold** l'or jaune
yes oui
yesterday hier
you're welcome de rien
young jeune
youth hostel l'auberge de jeunesse

Z

zoo le zoo

A

à droite right (direction)
à gauche left (direction)
l'abbaye abbey
abîmer v damage
accéder v access
accepter v accept
l'accès Wi-Fi wireless internet
accessible aux handicapés
handicapped- [disabled- BE]
accessible
l'accident accident
l'accompagnement side dish
d'accord OK
accueillir v welcome
acheter v buy
l'acuponcture acupuncture
l'adaptateur adapter
l'addition bill (check)
l'adresse address; ~ **mail** e-mail
address
l'aéroport airport
les affaires business
l'âge age
l'agence agency; ~ **de voyage**
travel agency
l'aide n help
aider v help
aimer v like (someone); ~ v love
(someone)
l'aire de jeux playground;
~ **de sport** field (sports)
l'aire de pique-nique picnic area

allaiter v breastfeed
l'allée aisle (theater)
aller v go (somewhere)
l'aller simple one-way
(ticket)
allergique allergic;
~ **au lactose** lactose intolerant
l'aller-retour round-trip
[return BE]
allumer v light (cigarette);
~ v turn on (lights)
l'ambulance ambulance
américain American
l'ami friend
amour n love
l'ampoule lightbulb
anémique anemic
l'anesthésie anesthesia
anglais British; English
l'animal animal
l'année year
l'anniversaire birthday
annuler v cancel
l'antibiotique antibiotic
l'antiquaire antique store
l'appareil photo camera;
~ **numérique** digital camera
l'appartement apartment
l'appel phone call
appeler v call
l'appendice appendix
(body part)
apporter v bring

après after
l'après after; ~-midi **afternoon;**
   ~-rasage **aftershave;**
   ~-shampooing **conditioner**
l'arbre tree
la salle de jeux arcade
l'argent money; ~ fin **sterling**
   silver
l'aromathérapie aromatherapy
arracher v extract (tooth)
l'arrêt n stop; ~ de bus **bus stop**
arrêter v stop
les arrivées arrivals (airport)
arriver v arrive
l'art arts
l'artère artery
l'arthrite arthritis
l'articulation joint
   (body part)
l'ascenseur elevator
   [lift BE]
asiatique Asian
l'aspirateur vacuum cleaner
l'aspirine aspirin
l'assiette plate
l'assurance insurance
asthmatique asthmatic
l'attaque attack
attaquer v mug
atteindre v reach
attendre v wait
l'attente n wait
au coin on/around the
   corner
au revoir goodbye
l'auberge de jeunesse
youth hostel
aujourd'hui today
l'Australie Australia
australien Australian
automatique automatic
l'autoroute highway
   [motorway BE]
avaler v swallow
l'avance cash advance
avant before
avec with
l'avion airplane
l'avocat lawyer
avoir v have; ~ besoin
   v need; ~ des vertiges
   dizzy; ~ la nausée **nauseous;**
   ~ un accident v crash (car)

B

le baby-sitter babysitter
le bagage à main carry-on
   [piece of hand luggage BE]
le bagage luggage
   [baggage BE]
la bague ring
les baguettes chopsticks
le balai broom
le ballet ballet
la banque bank
le bar bar (place), snack bar;
   ~ gay **gay bar**
le barbecue barbecue
la barque rowboat
bas low
le baseball baseball
le basketball basketball

le bateau boat; ~ **à moteur** motor boat
le bâtiment building
les bâtons poles (skiing)
beau attractive, beautiful
le bébé baby
le bed and breakfast bed and breakfast
beige beige
belle pretty
le berceau crib
le biberon baby bottle
la bibliothèque library
la bicyclette bicycle
bien well; ~ **reposé** well-rested
le bijou jewelry
la bijouterie jeweler
le bikini bikini
la billeterie ticket office; ~ **électronique** e-ticket
blanc white
bleu blue
boire v drink
la boisson n drink
la boîte box; ~-**à-lettres** mailbox [postbox BE]
bon adj good; ~ **après-midi** good afternoon; ~**marché** cheap
le bonbon candy [sweet BE]
bonjour hello, good morning
bonsoir good evening
les bottes boots
la bouche mouth
le boucher butcher

les boucles d'oreille earrings
la boulangerie bakery
la bouteille bottle
la boutique photo camera store
le bracelet bracelet
le bras arm
le briquet lighter
la broche brooch
la brosse hairbrush
brûler v burn
la buanderie laundry facility
le bureau office; ~ **de change** currency exchange office; ~ **de poste** post office; ~ **des renseignements** information desk; ~ **de réservation** reservation desk
le bus bus; ~ **direct** express bus

C

ça that
le cabaret cabaret
la cabine cabin; ~ **d'essayage** fitting [changing BE] room
le cachet tablet (medicine)
le cadeau gift
le cadenas n lock
le café café, coffee shop
la caisse cashier
les kilocalories calories
camper v camp
le camping campsite
le Canada Canada
canadien Canadian

la carafe carafe
le carrousel conveyor belt
la carte map, card;
~ **d'assurance** insurance card;
~ **des boissons** drink menu;
~ **de la chambre** key card;
~ **de crédit** credit card;
~ **d'embarquement**
boarding pass;
~ **internationale d'étudiant**
international student card;
~ **grise** vehicle registration;
~ **de membre** membership card;
~ **mémoire** memory card;
~ **des pistes** trail [piste BE] map;
~ **postale** postcard;
~ **de retrait** ATM/debit card;
~ **routière** road map;
~ **de téléphone** phone card;
~ **de la ville** town map;
~ **de visite** business card
la carte des vins wine list
la cartouche (de cigarettes)
carton (of cigarettes)
le cas case (amount)
la cascade waterfall
le casino casino
le casque helmet
cassé broken
casser v break (tooth, bone)
la casserole pot, saucepan
la cathédrale cathedral
la cave cave, cellar (wine)
le CD (disque compact) CD
ce soir tonight
ceci this

la ceinture belt
cela that
célibataire single (unmarried)
le cellophane plastic wrap
[cling film BE]
Celsius Celsius
le centimètre centimeter
centre center; ~ **commercial**
shopping mall [centre BE];
~ **d'affaires** business center; ~
ville town square; ~**-ville**
downtown area
le certificat certificate
la chaîne key ring, chain
la chaise chair; ~ **haute**
highchair; ~ **longue** deck chair; ~
roulante wheelchair
le chambranle display window/
case
la chambre simple single room
le champ field; ~ **de bataille**
battleground; ~ **la piste de**
course horsetrack
le change n exchange (place)
changer v change (baby)
le chapeau hat
le charbon de bois charcoal
la charcuterie delicatessen
le chariot cart [trolley BE]
le château castle
chaud hot, warm (temperature)
le chauffage heat (indoor)
le chauffage heater
la chaussette sock
les chaussons slippers
les chaussures shoes; ~ **de ski**

snowshoes; **~ à talons aiguilles**
high-heeled shoes; **~ de marche**
hiking boots; **~ plates** flat shoes
le chemin trail, path;
~ de randonnée walking route
la chemise shirt
le chemisier blouse
le chèque *n* check [cheque BE]
(payment); **~ de voyages**
traveler's check [cheque BE]
cher expensive
les cheveux hair
la cheville ankle
le chewing-gum chewing gum
le chien d'aveugle guide dog
chinois Chinese
le cigare cigar
la cigarette cigarette
le cinéma movie theater
les ciseaux scissors
la classe class; **~ affaire**
business class; **~ économique**
economy class
la clé key
la climatisation air conditioning
le club club; **~ gay** gay club;
~ de jazz jazz club
le code code; **~ national** country
code; **~ régional** area code;
~ secret personal identification
number (PIN)
le cœur heart
le coffre-fort safe (receptacle)
le coiffeur hair salon
le coiffeur pour hommes
barber

le col rond crew neck
le col en V V-neck
le colis package
le collègue colleague
le collier necklace
la colline hill
la colonne vertébrale spine
(body part)
combien how much
commander *v* order
commencer *v* begin
comment how
le commissariat de police
police station
la compagnie aérienne airline
la compagnie d'assurance
insurance company
composer *v* dial
comprendre *v* understand
le compte account; **~ courant**
checking [current BE] account;
~ épargne savings account
le concert concert
conduire *v* drive
la conférence conference
confirmer *v* confirm
le congélateur freezer
la congestion congestion
se connecter *v* connect (internet)
la connexion connection
(internet, telephone)
les conserves canned goods
la consigne luggage locker
la consigne locker
constipé constipated
le consulat consulate

le consultant consultant
contacter v contact
contagieux contagious
le contraire opposite
la contravention fine
  (fee for breaking law)
le contrôle de passeport
  passport control
  la correspondance change
  (buses); ~ **connection** (flight);
  ~ v transfer (change trains/flights)
le costume suit
la côte rib (body part)
le coton cotton
la couche diaper
  [nappy BE]
la couchette berth
le coude elbow
la couleur color
le couloir aisle (plane)
le cou neck
le coup de soleil sunburn
couper v cut
  la coupure bill [note BE] (money);
  ~ cut (injury)
le courrier mail [post BE];
  ~ **recommandé** registered mail
court short
le coût charge (cost)
le couteau knife
coûter v cost
le couvert cover charge
  (restaurant)
la couverture blanket
la cravate tie (clothing)
la crème cream/lotion;

~ **antiseptique** antiseptic cream;
~ **solaire** sunscreen
le cristal crystal
la cuillère spoon; ~ **à café**
  teaspoon; ~ **à doser**
  measuring spoon
le cuir leather
la cuisine kitchen
cuisiner v cook
la cuisse thigh
le cuivre copper
les culottes panties
le cyber café internet café

D

dangereux dangerous
dans in
dansant dancing
danser v dance
la date date (calendar)
de nuit overnight
de rien you're welcome
le déboucheur de
toilettes plunger
le débutant beginner
déclarer v declare
décoller v take off (plane)
déconnecter disconnect (computer)
le degré degree (temperature)
dehors outside
le déjeuner lunch
délicieux delicious
demain tomorrow
démarrer v start (an automobile)
demi half; ~-**heure** half hour;
  ~-**kilo** half-kilo

la dent tooth
la dentelle lace
le dentier denture
le dentifrice toothpaste
le dentiste dentist
le déodorant deodorant
la dépanneuse tow truck
les départs departures (airport)
déposer v deposit
le dépôt deposit (bank)
dernier last
derrière behind
descendre v get off
    (a train, bus, subway)
le désert desert
désolé sorry
le détergent detergent;
    ~ pour lave-vaisselle
    dishwashing liquid
développer v develop (film)
la déviation alternate route
diabétique diabetic
le diamant diamond
la diarrhée diarrhea
difficile difficult
dîner v dine; **le ~** dinner
la direction direction
la discothèque dance club;
disparu missing
disponible available
le disquaire music store
**le distributeur automatique de
billets** automatic teller machine
    (ATM)
le divertissement
    entertainment

divorcer v divorce
le docteur doctor
le doigt finger
le dollar dollar (U.S.)
donner v give
dormir v sleep
le dortoir dormitory
le dos back (body part)
la douane customs
doublé dubbed
la douche shower
la douleur hurt, pain;
    ~ à la poitrine chest pain
la douzaine dozen
le drap sheet
droit straight; **~ d'entrée** cover
    charge (bar, club)
du quartier local
DVD DVD

E

l'eau water; **~ chaude** hot
    water; **~ de Cologne** cologne;
    ~ potable drinking water
l'échange de monnaie currency
    exchange
échanger v change (money)
l'échantillon specimen
l'écharpe scarf
l'école school
les écouteurs headphones
l'écran solaire sunblock
écrire v text (send a message);
    ~ v write
effacer v clear (on an ATM)
l'effet secondaire side effect

l'effraction break-in (burglary)
égaliser trim (hair cut)
l'église church
l'émail enamel (jewelry)
emballer v wrap
embarquer v board
embrasser v kiss
emporter to go [take away BE] (food order)
en sécurité safe (protected)
encaisser v cash
enceinte pregnant
endommagé damaged
l'enfant child
enlacer v hug
ennuyant boring
l'enregistrement check-in (hotel, airport)
enregistrer v check (luggage)
ensoleillé sunny
l'entorse sprain
l'entrée admission; ~ appetizer [starter BE]; ~ entrance
entrer v enter
l'enveloppe envelope
envoyer v send, ship; ~ **un fax** v fax; ~ **un mail** v e-mail
l'épaule shoulder
épeler v spell
épicé hot (spicy)
l'épilation à la cire du maillot bikini wax
l'épilation à la cire des sourcils eyebrow wax
épileptique epileptic
l'épouse wife

épuisé exhausted
l'équipe team
l'équipement equipment; ~ **de plongée** diving/snorkeling equipment
l'erreur mistake
l'escalator escalators
les escaliers stairs
escarpé steep
ennuyer v bother
l'essence gas
l'essence petrol
est east
l'esthéticienne manicurist
l'estomac stomach
et and
l'étain pewter
l'étang pond
l'état de santé condition (medical); ~ **le problème cardiaque** heart condition
les États-Unis United States (U.S.)
éteindre v turn off (lights)
l'étiquette baggage ticket
étrange strange
être v be
l'étudiant student
étudier v study
l'euro euro
l'éventail fan (souvenir)
l'évier sink
l'excès excess
l'excursion excursion
excuser v excuse
l'expert expert (skill level)
l'express express

extra extra

F

facile easy
la facture bill [invoice BE]
faim hungry
faire v make, do; **~ des achats**
  v shop; **~ de l'auto stop**
  v hitchhike; **~ les bagages**
  v pack; **~ les courses**
  shopping; **~ le plein** v fill;
  se **~ réveiller par téléphone**
  wake-up call; **~ du**
tourisme sightseeing;
  ~ du vélo cycling;
  ~ de la vitesse speeding
faire un virement v transfer
  (money)
la falaise cliff
la famille family
le fast-food fast food
fatigué tired
le fax fax
la femme woman
la fenêtre window
le fer à repasser n iron
  (clothes)
fermé closed
la ferme farm
fermer v close, lock
le ferry ferry
les fesses buttocks
le feu fire; **~ tricolore** traffic light
fiancé engaged
la fièvre fever
la fille **girl**

le film movie
finir v end
la fleur flower
le foie liver (body part)
la fontaine fountain
le football soccer
  [football BE]
la forêt forest; **~ vierge**
  rainforest
le forfait lift pass
le formulaire form
le fort fort
la fourchette fork
frais cool (temperature); **~** fresh
français French
la France France
les freins brakes (car)
le frère brother
froid cold (temperature)
fumer v smoke

G

le garage garage, parking garage
garer v park
le garçon boy
la gare train [railway BE] station
la gare routière bus station
gay gay
le gaz cooking gas
la gazinière stove
le gazole diesel
le gel gel (hair)
le genou knee
le gilet de sauvetage life jacket
glacé icy
la glace ice

gonfler v swell
la gorge canyon; ~ throat
goûter v taste
la goutte drop (medicine)
le gramme gram
grand large
le grand magasin department store
grande taille plus size
les grands-parents
   grandparent
graver v engrave
gris gray
le groupe group
la gueule de bois hangover
le guide guide, guidebook
la gym gym
le gynécologue gynecologist

H

l'handicapé handicapped
   [disabled BE]
haut high
hebdomadaire weekly
l'hectare hectare
l'hétérosexuel heterosexual
l'heure hour
les heures d'ouverture
   business/office hours
les heures de visite visiting hours
heureux happy
hier yesterday
le hockey hockey; ~ **sur glace**
   ice hockey
l'homme man
l'hôpital hospital
l'horaire schedule [timetable BE]

hors taxe duty-free
l'hôtel hotel
l'huile oil

I

l'ibuprofène ibuprofen
ici here
l'identification identification
l'imperméable raincoat
imprimer v print
inclure v include
inconscient unconscious
infecté infected
l'infection vaginale
   vaginal infection
l'infirmier nurse
informer v notify
l'insecte bug
insérer v insert
l'insolation sunstroke
l'insomnie insomnia
l'insuline insulin
interdire v prohibit
intéressant interesting
l'international (terminal)
   international (airport area)
l'internet internet; ~ **sans
   fil** wireless internet
l'interprète interpreter
l'intersection intersection
l'intestin intestine
irlandais Irish
l'Irlande Ireland
l'irritation cutanée rash
italien Italian

J

la jambe leg
le jardin botanique botanical garden
jaune yellow
le jazz jazz
le jean jeans
jean denim
jetable disposable
le jeu game
jeune young
joindre v join
jouer v play
le jouet toy
le jour day
le journal newspaper
la jupe skirt

K

le kilo kilo; **~gramme** kilogram; **~métrage** mileage; **~mètre** kilometer; **~mètre carré** square kilometer
le kiosque à journaux newsstand
les Kleenex tissue

L

le lac lake
laid ugly
la laine wool
le lait pour bébés formula (baby)
la lame de rasoir razor blade
la lampe torche flashlight
la langue tongue
la laque hairspray

la laverie automatique laundromat [launderette BE]
le lave-vaisselle dishwasher
la leçon lesson
lentement slowly
les lentilles de contact contact lens
la lessive laundry
la lettre letter
les lèvres lip
la librairie bookstore
libre free; ~ vacancy
le lieu n place; **~ commémoratif** memorial (place); **~ saint** shrine; **~ touristique** attraction (place)
la ligne line (train)
la lime à ongle nail file
la lingette pour bébé baby wipe
le lin linen
le liquide n cash
le lit bed; ~ **double** double bed; **~ pliant** cot
le litre liter
le livre book
la livre sterling pounds (British sterling)
le logement accommodation
loin far
long long
la lotion anti-insectes insect repellent
louer v rent [hire BE]
la lumière light (overhead)
les lunettes glasses; **~ de soleil** sunglasses

M

la machine à laver
washing machine
la mâchoire jaw
le magasin store;
~ **de chaussures** shoe store;
~ **de jouets** toy store;
~ **de produits diététiques**
health food store;
~ **de souvenirs** souvenir store
~ **de sport** sporting goods store;
~ **de vêtements** clothing store;
~ **de vins et spiritueux**
liquor store
le magazine magazine
magnifique magnificent
le mail e-mail
le maillot de bain swimsuit
la main hand
maintenant now
la maison house
le mal sickness; ~ **de l'air**
motion -sickness (air); ~ **de dos**
backache; ~ **de gorge** sore throat;
~ **de mer** motion
sickness (sea); ~ **de tête**
headache; ~ **des transports**
travel sickness
malade ill, sick
les maladies sexuellement
transmissibles sexually
transmitted disease (STD)
malvoyant visually impaired
les manches courtes short sleeves
les manches longues long sleeves
manger v eat

le manteau coat
la manucure manicure
le marchand de fruits
et légumes produce store
le marchand de vins et de
spiritueux liquor store
[off-licence BE]
le marché market
marcher v walk
le mari husband
marié married
la mairie town hall
se marier v marry
marron brown
le marteau hammer
le massage massage
le match n match; ~ **de boxe**
boxing match; ~ **de football**
soccer [football BE] game; ~ **de**
volleyball volleyball game
le matin morning
le maux de ventre stomachache
le mécanicien mechanic
le médicament medicine
meilleur best
le même same
le menu menu; ~ **enfant**
children's menu
la mer sea
merci thank you
la mère mother
le message message;
~ **instantané** instant message
la messe mass (church service)
la mesure measuring cup
mesurer to measure (someone)

la météo forecast
le mètre carré square meter
le métro subway
[underground BE]
le micro-onde microwave
midi noon [midday BE]
mieux better
mignon cute
le mini bar mini-bar
minuit midnight
la minute minute
le mobile home mobile home
la mobilité mobility
la mobylette moped
les mocassins loafers
modifier v alter
moins less; **~ cher** cheaper
le mois month
la moitié half
la monnaie n change (money);
~ currency
la montagne mountain
la montre watch
montrer v show
le morceau piece
la mosquée mosque
le mot de passe password
la moto motorcycle
la mousse mousse; **~ à raser**
shaving cream
moyen medium (size)
le muscle muscle
le musée museum
la musique music; **~ classique**
classical music; **~ folklorique**
folk music

myope near- [short- BE] sighted

N

nager v swim
national domestic
la nationalité nationality
neigeux snowy
nettoyer v clean
le nez nose
le night club nightclub
le niveau intermédiaire
intermediate
noir black
le nom name; **~ de l'utilisateur**
username
non no; **~ alcoolisé**
non-alcoholic; **~ fumeur**
non-smoking
nord north
nourrir v feed
le novice novice
(skill level)
de nuit overnight
la nuit night
numérique digital
le numéro number; **~ de fax**
fax number; **~ de permis de**
conduire driver's license -number;
~ de téléphone
phone number

O

les objets trouvés lost and found
l'œil eye
l'oiseau bird
l'ongle fingernail, toenail

l'opéra opera
l'opticien optician
l'or gold; **~ blanc** white gold;
  ~ jaune yellow gold
orange orange (color)
l'orchestre orchestra
ordinaire regular
l'ordinateur computer
l'ordonnance prescription
les ordures à recycler recycling
l'oreille ear
l'oreiller pillow
l'orteil toe
l'os bone
l'otite earache
où where
ouest west
oui yes
ouvert open
l'ouvre-bouteille/boîte bottle/can
  opener
ouvrir v open; **~ une session** v log
  on (computer)

P

le palais palace
le palais des congrès
  -convention hall
le panier basket (grocery store)
la panne breakdown
le pansement bandage
le pantalon pants [trousers BE]
le papier paper; **~ aluminium**
  aluminum [kitchen BE] foil;
  ~ toilette toilet paper
le paquet carton

par by; **~ avion** airmail; **~ heure**
  per hour; **~ jour** per day; **~ nuit**
  per night; **~ semaine** per week
le paracétamol acetaminophen
  [paracetamol BE]
le parapluie umbrella
le parc playpen; **~ park;**
  ~ d'attractions amusement park
le parfum perfume
parier to place (a bet)
le parking parking lot
  [car park BE]
parler v speak
participer v attend
pas cher inexpensive
le passager passenger
le passeport passport
passer v pass through
la passoire colander
la pataugeoire kiddie pool
la pâtisserie pastry shop
payer v pay; **~ par carte**
  v charge (credit card)
la peau skin
le pédiatre pediatrician
la pédicure pedicure
le peigne comb
la pellicule film (camera)
pendant during
la pendule wall clock
la pénicilline penicillin
le pénis penis
perdre v lose (something)
perdu lost
le père father
la période period (of time)

la perle pearl
permettre v allow
la perte discharge (bodily fluid)
petit small
le petit child, small;
 ~-**ami** boyfriend;
 ~-**amie** girlfriend;
 ~ **déjeuner** breakfast
les petits-enfants grandchildren
peu little
la pharmacie pharmacy
 [chemist BE]
la photo photo; ~**copie**
 photocopy; ~**graphie**
 photography; ~ **numérique**
 digital photo
la pièce coin; ~ part (for car);
 ~ n play (theater); ~ room
le pied foot
le piéton pedestrian
la pile battery
le pilier tent pole
la pilule Pill (birth control)
le piquet tent peg
la piqûre sting; ~ **d'insecte**
 insect bite
la piscine pool; ~ **intérieure**
 indoor pool; ~ **extérieure**
 outdoor pool
la piste trail [piste BE]; ~ **cyclable**
 bike route
la pizzeria pizzeria
la plage beach
la plainte complaint
le plaisir pleasure
le plan du magasin store directory

le plat principal main course
platine platinum
le plombage filling (tooth)
plonger v dive
la pluie rain
plus more; ~ **bas** lower;
 ~ **fort** louder; ~ **grand** larger;
 ~ **lent** slower; ~ **petit** smaller;
 ~ **tard** later; ~ **tôt** earlier;
 ~ **vite** faster
pluvieux rainy
le pneu tire [tyre BE]; ~ **crevé**
 flat tire [tyre BE]
la poche pocket
la poêle frying pan
le poignet wrist
le point d'observation overlook
 [viewpoint BE] (scenic place)
le poison poison
la poitrine chest (body part)
la police police
la pompe à air air pump
les pompiers fire department
le pont bridge
la pop musique pop music
le portable wireless/cell
 [mobile BE] phone
la porte gate (airport); ~ door;
 ~ **coupe-feu** fire door
le portefeuille wallet
la portion portion; ~ **enfant**
 children's portion
la pose exposure (film)
le poste extension (phone)
le pot jar
la poterie pottery

le poubelle garbage [rubbish BE]
le poumon lung
la poupée doll
pour for
pourpre purple
pousser to push (door sign)
la poussette stroller
[pushchair BE]
précieux valuable
premier first
la première classe first class
prendre v pick up (something);
~ v take; ~ **plaisir** v enjoy;
~ **sa retraite** retired
près close, near; ~ **de** nearby
presbyte far- [long- BE] sighted
prescrire to prescribe
présenter v introduce
le préservatif condom
prévoir v schedule
la principale attraction
touristique main attraction
la prise électrique electric outlet
le prix price
le problème problem
produire produce
le produit product; ~
d'entretien cleaning product;
~ **ménager** household good
profondément deeply
la promenade walk
prononcer v pronounce
propre clean
public public
le pull sweater
le pyjama pajamas

Q

le quai n track [platform BE] (train)
la qualité quality
quand when
le quartier des magasins
shopping area
la question question
qui who
quitter la chambre check-out
(hotel)
quoi what

R

raccourcir v to shorten
la rampe d'accès wheelchair ramp
le rap rap (music)
le rapport de police police report
la raquette racket (sports)
le rasoir jetable disposable razor
la réaction allergique allergic
reaction
la réception reception
recevoir v receive
recharger v recharge
le réchaud camping stove
réchauffer v warm (something)
recommandation
recommendation
recommander v recommend
le reçu n bill, receipt (of sale)
recycler recycling
la réduction discount
le réfrigérateur refrigerator
refuser v decline (credit card)
regarder v look
la région region

les règles period (menstrual)
les règles douloureuses
  menstrual cramps
le rein kidney (body part)
la relation relationship
remercier v thank
le remonte-pentes drag lift
la remorque trailer
remplir v fill out (form)
rencontrer v meet (someone)
le rendez-vous appointment
rendre v return (something)
les renseignements information
  (phone)
réparer v fix (repair)
le repas meal
repasser v iron
répéter v repeat
la réservation reservation
la réserve naturelle nature preserve
réserver v reserve
le résident européen EU resident
respirer v breathe
le responsable manager
le restaurant restaurant
rester v stay
retarder v delay
retirer v withdraw
le retrait withdrawal (bank);
  ~ des bagages baggage claim
la réunion meeting
réveiller v wake
le rez-de-chaussée ground floor
le rhume cold (sickness)
rien anything, nothing
la rivière river

la robe dress (piece of clothing)
romantique romantic
rose pink
rouge red
la route route
le Royaume Uni United Kingdom
  (U.K.)
le rugby rugby
les ruines ruins
le ruisseau stream

S

s'asseoir v sit
s'il vous plaît please
le sac bag, purse; **~ à dos**
  backpack; **~ à appareil photo**
  camera case; **~ de couchage**
  sleeping bag; **~ à main** purse
  [handbag BE]; **~ poubelle**
  garbage [rubbish BE] bag
le sachet bag
saigner v bleed
le saladier bowl
sale dirty
la salle room:
  ~ d'attente waiting room;
  ~ de concert concert hall;
  ~ à manger dining room;
  ~ de réunion meeting room
le salon d'essayage fitting room
salut hi
les sandales sandals
le sang blood
sans without; **~ 0% de matières**
  grasses fat free; **~ ordonnance**
  over the counter (medication);

~ **plomb** unleaded (gasoline); ~
surveillance unattended
la santé health
Santé! Cheers!
le sauna sauna
sauvegarder v save (computer)
le savon soap
le scanner scanner
la science science
le sèche-cheveux hair dryer
le secouriste lifeguard
la sécurité security
le sein breast
le self-service self-service
la semaine week
le séminaire seminar
les seniors senior citizens
le sens unique one-way street
séparé separated (marriage)
sérieux serious
la serpillière mop;
~ groundcloth
le serveur waiter
la serveuse waitress
le service service (in a restaurant);
~ **de chambre** room service;
~ **complet** full-service;
~ **d'entretien** housekeeping
services; ~ **internet** internet
service; ~ **de nettoyage**
laundry service
la serviette napkin, towel;
~ **hygiénique** sanitary napkin
[pad BE]
seul alone
seulement only

le shampooing shampoo
le short shorts
le siège seat; ~ **bébé** car seat;
~ **couloir** aisle seat;
~ **enfant** child's seat
signer v sign
le silence quiet
le ski ski; ~ **jet** jet ski
skier v ski
les skis nautiques water skis
les slips briefs [underpants BE]
(clothing)
le snowboard snowboard
la sœur sister
la soie silk
soif thirsty
le soin à l'oxygène oxygen
treatment
le soin du visage facial
la soirée evening
le sol floor
le soleil sun
**la solution pour lentilles de
contact** contact lens solution
sombre dark
le sommet peak
somnolence drowsiness
la serviette en papier paper towel
la sortie exit; ~ **de secours**
emergency exit
sortir to exit
la source chaude hot spring
sourd deaf
les sous-vêtements underwear
le soutien-gorge bra
le souvenir souvenir

le spa spa
la spatule spatula
le spécialiste specialist (doctor)
le sport sports
le stade stadium
la station station; ~ **de métro** subway [underground BE] station; ~ **service** gas [petrol BE] station
la statue statue
stupéfiant stunning
le style de coiffure hairstyle
le stylo pen
subtil subtitle
sucré sweet (taste)
sud south
suivant next
le super super (fuel)
supérieur upper
le supermarché supermarket
la supervision supervision
supprimer v delete (computer)
le surf surfboard
surprenant amazing
le sweat-shirt sweatshirt
le symbole symbol (keyboard)
la synagogue synagogue
le syndicat d'initiative tourist information office
le Syndrome d'immunodéficience acquise (SIDA) AIDS

T

le tabac tobacconist
la table table
la taille size

le tampon tampon
frapper v (computer) type
le tapis de sol groundcloth
tard late (time)
la tasse cup
le taux de change exchange rate
la taxe duty (tax)
le taxi taxi
la teinturerie dry cleaner
la télé TV; ~**le téléphérique** cable car; ~**le téléphone** phone; ~**le téléphone public** pay phone
téléphoner v phone
le télésiège chair lift
le temple temple (religious)
temporaire temporary
le temps time, weather; ~ **partiel** part-time; ~ **plein** full-time
le tennis tennis
les tennis sneakers
la tension blood pressure
la tente tent
la tenue exigée dress code
le terminal terminal (airport)
terminer une session v log off (computer)
le terrain field, course; ~ **de golf** golf course
la terre cuite terracotta
terrible terrible
la tête head (body part)
la tétine pacifier [soother BE]
le texte text (message)
le théâtre theater
le ticket ticket; ~ **de bus** bus ticket
le timbre stamp (postage)

le tirage unique single prints
le tire-bouchon corkscrew
tirer v pull (door sign)
les toilettes restroom [toilet BE]
les toilettes portables
   chemical toilet
tôt early
total total (amount)
la tour tower
le touriste tourist
le tournoi de golf golf tournament
tousser v cough
tout de suite right of way
la toux cough
traditionnel traditional
traduire v translate
le train train
tranchant sharp
la tranche slice
travailler v work
très grand extra large
triste sad
trop too
le t-shirt T-shirt
la TVA sales tax [VAT BE]

U

un one
une fois once
l'université university
l'urgence emergency
urgent urgent
l'ustensile utensil
les produits d'entretien
   cleaning supplies
utiliser v use

V

les vacances vacation
[holiday BE]
la vaccination vaccination
le vagin vagina
la vaisselle dish (kitchen)
la valeur value
valide valid
la valise suitcase
la vallée valley
végétarien vegetarian
le véliplanchiste windsurfer
le vélo tout terrain (VTT)
   mountain bike
vendre v sell
venir v come
le ventilateur fan (appliance)
vérifier v check (on something)
le verre glass, lens
vert green
la vessie bladder
la veste jacket
les vêtements clothing
le veuf widowed
vider v empty
vieux old
le vignoble vineyard
le village village
la ville town
le viol rape
violer v rape
le visage face
la visite tour; ~ **en bus** bus tour
la visite touristique sightseeing
   tour
visiter v visit

itamine vitamin
fast
itrine display case
e v live
v see
oiture car; **~ automatique**
utomatic car; **~ de location**
ar rental [hire BE]; **~ de location**
ental [hire BE] car; **~ manuelle**
anual car
ol flight; **~ theft**; **~ national**
omestic flight; **~ international**
ternational flight
~ stolen
er v rob, steal

le voleur thief
vomir v vomit
le voyage trip
vrai real

W

le wagon couchette sleeper
[sleeping BE] car
le week-end weekend
wireless internet wireless internet
service

Z

la zone fumeur smoking (area)
le zoo zoo

Berlitz®

speaking your language

phrase book & dictionary
phrase book & CD

Available in: Arabic, Brazilian Portuguese*, Burmese*, Cantonese
Chinese, Croatian, Czech*, Danish*, Dutch, English, Filipino, Finnish*, French,
German, Greek, Hebrew*, Hindi*, Hungarian*, Indonesian, Italian, Japanese,
Korean, Latin American Spanish, Malay, Mandarin Chinese, Mexican Spanish,
Norwegian, Polish, Portuguese, Romanian*, Russian, Spanish, Swedish, Thai,
Turkish, Vietnamese
*Book only